TIBETAN ARTS OF LOVE

TIBETAN ARTS OF LOVE

Gedün Chöpel

Introduced and Translated by Jeffrey Hopkins
With Dorje Yudon Yuthok

Snow Lion Publications
Ithaca, New York USA

Snow Lion Publications
P. O. Box 6483
Ithaca, New York 14851
USA

Printed in USA

ISBN 0-937938-97-1 Paper

Library of Congress Cataloging-in-Publication Data

Dge-'dun-chos-'phel, A-mdo, 1905?-1951?
   ['Dod pa'i bstan bcos. English]
   Tibetan arts of love / Gedun Chöpel ; translated by Jeffrey
Hopkins with Dorje Yuthok.
      p.   cm.
   Translation of: 'Dod pa 'i bstan bcos.
   ISBN 0-937938-97-1
   1. Sex instruction—Religious Aspects—Buddhism.   2. Sex-
-Religious aspects—Buddhism.   3. Buddhism—China—Tibet.
I. Hopkins, Jeffrey.   II. Yuthok, Dorje Yudon, 1912-   .
III. Title.
HQ56.D4413   1992
306.7'0951'5—dc20   91-25858
                                                        CIP

Contents

Preface

In 1967 near the end of my five-year stay at the Lamaist Buddhist Monastery of America in Freewood Acres, New Jersey, Mrs. Dorje Yudon Yuthok asked me to translate brief notes that later, upon extensive revision and expansion with others' help, became her autobiography, published in 1990 as *House of the Turquoise Roof*.[1] When we finished, she indicated that an English version of Gedün Chöpel's *Treatise on Passion* might be useful in the West, and so we began a translation. There were many problematic passages in the 1967 edition of the Tibetan text, and the manuscript sat for twenty-four years among unfinished projects. In the meantime I procured a much better edition (the 1983 reprint of the edited 1969 edition)[2] and in 1991 began a re-translation, which has resulted in this publication.

Some translations of erotica in the past have suffered from the intrusion of the views of the translators into

---

[1] Ithaca: Snow Lion Publications.

[2] For discussion of the editions, see p. 152.

the text, usually by omitting what is imagined to be sensitive material. The reader can be assured that this translation attempts to be an utterly accurate and all-inclusive (unexpurgated!) rendition of the original. The chapter titles are taken from Gedün Chöpel's own indication of the contents at the end of sections, with the exception of the titles of chapters one through five and chapter nine which were added from context. The title of chapter eighteen is found in a table of contents at the beginning of the two editions of the Tibetan text in India but not in the text itself. Internal headings have been added for the sake of accessibility.

The names of Tibetan authors and orders are given in 'essay phonetics' for the sake of easy pronunciation; for a discussion of the system used, see the Technical Note at the beginning of Jeffrey Hopkins, *Meditation on Emptiness* (London: Wisdom Publications, 1983), pp. 19-22. Transliteration of Tibetan is done in accordance with a system devised by Turrell Wylie; see 'A Standard System of Tibetan Transcription', *Harvard Journal of Asiatic Studies*, Vol. 22, 1959, pp. 261-7. For Indian names used in the body of the text, *ch*, *sh*, and *ṣh* are used instead of the more usual *c*, *ś*, and *ṣ* for the sake of easy pronunciation by non-specialists.

I wish to thank Professors David White and Donald Lopez for making many suggestions that improved the translation.

Jeffrey Hopkins
University of Virginia

Introduction

by Jeffrey Hopkins

1 Gedün Chöpel: Provocative Iconoclast

Gedün Chöpel's *Treatise on Passion* presents with evocative clarity the sixty-four arts of love mentioned, but not elaborated in equivalent detail, in the world-famous *Kāma Sūtra* of India. Thus, this book is particularly useful to persons who wish to enhance the intimacy and impact of sexual play. Equally important is the underlying theme of the book, the compatibility of sexual pleasure with spiritual insight. In Tantric Buddhism the sixty-four arts of love are deliberately used in a process of spiritual development in order to enhance the state of ecstatic orgasm that brings with it manifestation of a more subtle and powerful level of consciousness. Since this consciousness can reveal the nature of reality with tremendous force, it has dynamic import for the spiritual path. Gedün Chöpel makes frequent reference to the spiritual value of sexual pleasure, and thus this book, while presenting copious advice on how to enhance ordinary sex, also indicates a higher type of love practiced in Indo-Tibetan Tantrism.

In addition, the book contains numerous statements

about the appropriate lifestyle for a person to follow in a culture, like that of Tibet, which advocates celibacy for a large part of the population. These passages can be viewed as the author's analysis of his own situation as a person who gave up the vows of monkhood, but they also can be seen as providing a Buddhist ethic of how to live with one's desires. In addition, Gedün Chöpel gives numerous prescriptions for men to treat women as true partners; thus, despite his concessions to the sexist preference in Tibetan culture for male progeny—indicating how to insure male offspring—the text speaks with intimate concern for the sexual pleasure of women and how to achieve it.

THE AUTHOR

Gedün Chöpel[1] was born Rik-dzin-ñam-gyel[2] in 1905[3] in

---

[1] *dge 'dun chos 'phel.*

[2] *rig 'dzin rnam rgyal.*

[3] My sources for the author's biography are:

- Heather Stoddard, *Le mendiant de L'Amdo*, Recherches sur la Haute Asie 9 (Paris: Société d'Ethnographie, 1985).
- K. Dhondup, "Gedun Chophel: The Man Behind the Legend", *Tibetan Review*, vol. xiii no. 10, October, 1978, 10-18.
- Heather Karmay (alias Heather Stoddard), "dGe-'dun Chos-'phel, the artist" in *Tibetan Studies in Honour of Hugh Richardson*, ed. Michael Aris and Aung San Suu Kyi (Warminster, Wiltshire: Aris and Phillips Ltd., 1980).
- D. Seyfort Ruegg, "A Tibetan Odyssey: A Review Article", *Journal of the Royal Asiatic Society*, no. 2, 1989, pp. 304-311.
- La-chung-a-po (*bla chung a pho*), in *Biographical Dictionary of Tibet and Tibetan Buddhism*, compiled by Khetsun Sangpo (Dharamsala: Library of Tibetan Works and Archives, 1973), vol. 5, 634-657, with oral commentary (tape recorded) from Khetsun Sangpo. La-chung-a-po first met Gedün Chöpel after his return to Hla-sa in 1945, after which they became very close friends. He wrote the biography in 1972.
- Melvyn C. Goldstein, *A History of Modern Tibet, 1913-1951;*

by the name of Father Griebenow who lived for a number of years in a town on the outskirts of the monastery and who gave him some ideas for the boat. In 1927, in his twenties, under pressure from his college at Dra-shi-kyil over critical remarks he made about the college's textbooks, he transferred to central Tibet to the Go-mang[1] College of Dre-bung[2] Monastic University on the outskirts of Hla-sa. At Go-mang he became a student of the influential scholar Shay-rap-gya-tso,[3] an associate of the Thirteenth Dalai Lama who after the Communist takeover became Chairman of the All China Buddhist Association and Vice President of Ch'ing-hai Province. Both teacher and student were active personalities, and Gedün Chöpel frequently contested Shay-rap-gya-tso's teachings. Gedün Chöpel—whom his teacher called not by his name but by the epithet "madman"—gave up attending his classes. About this he said, "Though Shay-rap pretends to teach texts to me, he is not at all my equal. I refute whatever he says; we always slip into debate. Aside from calling me 'madman', he doesn't call me by my name."[4]

He was fond of provoking other scholars in debate. Once he came to the debating courtyard dressed up as an illiterate monk-policeman, challenging and defeating the Mongolian scholar Ngak-wang-lek-den,[5] who later became abbot of Go-mang. On another occasion he

---

[1] *sgo mang.*
[2] *'bras spungs.*
[3] *shes rab rgya mtsho; c.* 1884-1968.
[4] *La-chung-a-po,* 637.
[5] *ngag dbang legs ldan.* This is not the Tibetan scholar whose teachings I translated in "Meditations of a Tantric Abbot" in Tsong-ka-pa, Kensur Lekden, and Jeffrey Hopkins, *Compassion in Tibetan Buddhism* (London: Rider and Company, 1980; rpt. Ithaca: Snow Lion, 1980), pp. 15-79. Stoddard (151) later mistakenly refers to the latter (who became the abbot of the Tantric College of Lower Hla-sa) as also a Mongol.

took such an unusual position against the chief scholar of Go-mang's rival college within Dre-bung Monastic University, called Lo-sel-ling,[1] that his opponent was reduced to silence. He even took the position that Buddhahood does not exist, with the result that an irate group of monks beat him up and with brute force made him agree that indeed Buddhahood does exist. The story says a great deal about the power of group-control that set limits on the analytical probings in Ge-luk-ba colleges. Gedün Chöpel appears not to have always employed the usual facades through which Tibetan scholars pretend that their highly critical analyses are only clarifications, and not revisions or refutations, of famous figures' opinions. He apparently paid little attention to his studies while at Go-mang and left just before he was to take exams for the ge-shay degree, eschewing the vanity of high position.

Gedün Chöpel was fond of drawing, making sketches both while at Go-mang as a means to "fill his belly"[2] and while traveling with Rahula Sankrityayana (1893-1963) north of Hla-sa in 1934 to search for Sanskrit manuscripts and to the important Buddhist pilgrimage sites of southern Tibet, Nepal, and India. Rahula Sankrityayana, who became a life-long friend, was a Sanskrit scholar who worked in the Indian independence movement; he was a member of the Communist Party of India and often traveled to Russia. Gedün Chöpel accompanied him on a return-expedition to Tibet for six months in 1938, after which he was employed at the Bihar Research Society in Patna, not returning to Tibet until 1945. Heather Stoddard relates a story from the expedition photographer, Fany

---

[1] *blo gsal gling.*
[2] Karmay, 146.

Mukerjee:[1]

> We used to talk about art a lot. I was educated in the western tradition in which art is one activity that can be picked up at a moment's notice and put down again, but Gedün Chöpel said the most important thing is concentration. The mind must be totally absorbed in the subject. One day for a joke he said that he would show me what he meant. He went to the market and bought a bottle of arak [liquor], he started to drink. He drank and drank and kept asking whether this face had gone red yet. By the last drop he was quite inebriated. He stripped off stark naked and sat down and started to draw; he drew a perfect figure of a man starting off at one fingertip and going all round in one continuous line until he ended back up at the fingertip again.

This single story conveys a sense of Gedün Chöpel's interest in liquor, sex, meditation, and art.

In Kalimpong he worked with Tar-chin Babu-la[2] to compile a Tibetan-English dictionary that includes a little Hindi. Tar-chin Babu-la provided a meeting place for many reform-minded but frustrated young Tibetans. Among these were:

- Rap-ga Ḅom-da-tsang,[3] an important leader from the southeastern province of Tibet called Kam[4] who had political and financial links with the Chinese Guomindang. He translated some of Sun Yat-sen's writings into Tibetan.

---

[1] Karmay, 198. I have used my essay phonetic spelling of the author's name in order to avoid confusion.

[2] *mthar phyin bha bu lags*, 1890-1976.

[3] *rab dga' spom mda' tshang*, 1902-1979.

[4] *khams*.

- Ba-ba Pün-tsok-wang-gyel,[1] a true Tibetan Communist, who presented a plan for reform to the Tibetan government in 1949 and who subsequently assumed high office in the Chinese government. He was jailed during the cultural revolution, and finally was rehabilitated in 1979.[2]

- Tup-den-gün-pel-la, [3] the favored attendant of the Thirteenth Dalai Lama who was so influential that he was described as, next to the Dalai Lama, the most powerful person in Tibet.[4] He was exiled in 1934 after the Dalai Lama's death by those jealous of his power; the day chosen for his banishment was the twenty-ninth day of the twelfth month of the Tibetan calendar—the day when all the evil forces of the past year are ritually gathered together and banished. He was brought to the center of Hla-sa and forced to pass by his father who had been arrested and brought from the opposite direction; they were not allowed to

---

[1] *'ba' pa phun tshogs dbang rgyal.*

[2] In 1986 I met him at his apartment in Beijing. I expected to find a white-haired old man and was surprised to see a vigorous black-haired, almost athletic man. I had come with a Mongolian tour-guide in order to provide someone who could report to the Chinese government what transpired, and Pün-tsok-wang-gyel was very careful to translate into Chinese everything we said in Tibetan. Although the tense suspicion could be cut with a knife, we had a delightful conversation while eating pears. He said that I was the first Westerner who spoke Tibetan with whom he had contact, and he seemed to enjoy the meeting. I presented him with a copy of the Dalai Lama's *Kindness, Clarity, and Insight*, and he stared at the picture on the front as if to try to reinstate contact with his old friend. When we parted, he happily announced that he had been honored finally to meet with Karl Marx; I was startled, but he motioned with his hand to his chin to indicate that he was making a joke about my big beard (and probably also my large forehead). I outwardly laughed and inwardly was amused at the fact that one of the Dalai Lama's nicknames for me was "Marx" for the same reason.

[3] *thub bstan kun 'phel lags;* born around 1905.

[4] Goldstein, *A History of Modern Tibet,* 151.

speak to each other as they passed—an act of exquisitely crafted cruelty.

These persons were all interested in improving and modernizing conditions in Tibet in an atmosphere intolerant of change and dissent that was exacerbated by British maneuverings to maintain its dominance in India. It seems to me that their common nationalism was stronger than their Guomindang or Communist affiliations, and it is unfortunate that intolerance for pluralism, intensified by fear of foreign domination, did not allow the Tibetan government and people to benefit from these leaders' vision and energy.

Gedün Chöpel began learning English in Sikkim from an old Christian nun. With more instruction from a Sikkimese he passed a matriculation exam after just six months. With the nun, he traveled to Kulu in India at the request of George Roerich (1902-1961), a Russian political fugitive and scholar of Tibet, Mongolia, and Buddhism, where he and the nun translated into English Dharmakīrti's very abstruse *Commentary on (Dignāga's) "Compendium of [Teachings on] Valid Cognition"*.[1] Gedün Chöpel also helped Roerich with the English translation of the important fifteenth-century history of Tibetan Buddhism, the *Blue Annals*.[2]

Gedün Chöpel studied Pāli at the Kashi Vidyapith School and Sanskrit at Benaras with Ku-nu La-ma Dendzin-gyel-tsen,[3] who reported that Gedün Chöpel was so sharp that he could memorize in a day a Sanskrit text that took him weeks to memorize. Gedün Chöpel translated Kalidasa's *Shakuntala*, the *Rāmāyaṇa*, chapter twelve of the *Bhagavad Gītā* (in collaboration with Swami

---

[1] *tshad ma rnam 'grel gyi tshig le'ur byas pa, pramāṇavārttikakārikā*; P5709, vol. 130. The whereabouts of the translation is unknown.

[2] *deb ther sngon po*. See George N. Roerich, trans. (Delhi: Motilal Banarsidass, rpt. 1979).

[3] *khu nu bla ma bstan 'dzin rgyal mtshan*.

Prabhandananda), a long section of the Vedas, and parts of the *Udānavarga* from Sanskrit into Tibetan. He translated the entire *Dhammapada* from Pāli into Tibetan, translated the chapter on wisdom in Shāntideva's *Engaging in the Bodhisattva Deeds* from Sanskrit into English, and translated British military commands into Tibetan (at the request of the Tibetan government). He wrote philosophical texts in Tibetan, including presentations of the Mind Only School, difficult points on reasoning, and non-Buddhist philosophies. He also wrote four texts on medicine as well as long works on his voyages and guidebooks.[1]

In the winter of 1945, after roughly a total of thirteen years in India and sixteen months in Sri Lanka (he was tremendously impressed with the life-style of the older Sri Lankan monks), Gedün Chöpel returned to Hla-śa. There, he worked with the Buriat Mongol Chö-drak to compile one of the best modern dictionaries of Tibetan, and with patronage from the great noble house of Hor-kang[2] he published an early Tibetan history called *White Annals.*[3]

In Hla-śa, he also taught Mādhyamika philosophy with his own highly controversial interpretation. His student, the Ñying-ma-ba Da-wa-sang-bo,[4] took notes during these teachings, and along with Gedün Chöpel's earlier composition on the topic of valid cognition (written on a note pad) he compiled these into a book entitled *Good Explanation Distilling the Profound Essentials*

---

[1] For a complete list of his works, see Stoddard, 329-336.

[2] *hor khang.*

[3] *deb ther dkar po.* For an English translation, see Gedun Choephel, *The White Annals*, translated by Samten Norboo (Dharamsala: Library of Tibetan Works and Archives, 1978). He is said to have written histories of India and Ceylon with illustrations, but these have not survived.

[4] *zla ba bzang po.*

of the Middle: Ornament for the Thought of Nāgārjuna.[1] It was published in Hla-ša[2] and then in Kalimpong in 1951. The work is critical of the interpretation of Mādhyamika philosophy by Dzong-ka-ba Lo-sang-drak-ba,[3] who was the founder of the Ge-luk-ba order and thus the chief object of sectarian allegiance at both of Gedün Chöpel's monastic universities, Dra-ši-kyil in Am-do and Dre-bung Go-mang at Hla-ša. Gedün Chöpel warned Da-wa-sang-bo that after his death, the book would give rise to controversy and that he should take care.

An Inner Mongolian scholar, Ge-šhay Gel-den,[4] who took up residence in New Jersey, told me that he met a drunken Gedün Chöpel once on the streets of Hla-ša. Gedün Chöpel took him inside a house and with great lucidity laid out his interpretation of Mādhyamika. Ge-šhay Gel-den was amazed at his clarity despite being inebriated, a feat similar to the earlier demonstration of his powers of concentration by drawing when intoxi-cated.

Gedün Chöpel's basic criticism of Dzong-ka-ba's intri-cate analysis of Mādhyamika is of being over-subtle. Specifically, he found Dzong-ka-ba's distinction between existence and inherent existence and the claim that only inherent existence is refuted in emptiness is too ab-struse.[5] Indeed, Dzong-ka-ba holds that until one real-izes emptiness, one cannot validly distinguish between

---

[1] *dbu ma'i zab gdad snying por dril ba'i legs bshad klu sgrub dgongs rgyan* (Kalimpong: Mani Printing Works, 1951; also: bod ljongs bod yig dpe rnying dpe skrun khang, 1990. Professor Donald Lopez is cur-rently preparing a translation and study of this work.

[2] Stoddard (332) mentions an undated xylographic edition in Hla-ša. La-chung-a-po (647.15) says it was published under the patron-age of Ga-šhö-ba (*ka shod pa*).

[3] *tsong kha pa blo bzang grags pa*; 1357-1419.

[4] *dge bshes skal ldan.*

[5] 290.8. All citations are to the *bod ljongs bod yig dpe rnying dpe skrun khang* edition.

existence and inherent existence, and yet he insists that
the first step in meditation on emptiness is to get a clear
idea of what inherent existence is and how it appears to
the mind. Ḍzong-ka-ḅa's followers attempt to explain
away the apparent discrepancy by holding that the initial identification of inherent existence is with a mere
correct assumption and not with valid cognition.
Nevertheless, Gedün Chöpel's criticism emphasizes
the need to realize emptiness in meditation and not be
content with verbal manipulation of terminology the
meaning of which has not been experienced. He therefore concludes that no matter what verbal distinctions
are made, one has in fact to refute pot, pillar, existence,
non-existence, and so forth themselves—not making
the mistake of leaving the basic object as it is and seeking to refute some separate inherent existence. He
identifies this as the system of both the Ñying-ma-ḅas
and of experientially based Ge-luk-ḅa scholars such as
Jang-ḡya Röl-ḅay-dor-jay,[1] Gung-tang Ḡön-chok-ḍen-
ḅay-drön-may,[2] and the First Paṇ-chen Lama Ḷo-sang -
chö-ḡyi-gyel-tsen.[3] As Jang-ḡya says:[4]

> It seems that leaving these concrete appearances
> as they are, they are searching for some horn-
> like thing to refute.

Hence, Gedün Chöpel was objecting not to Ge-luk-ḅa
scholarship in general but to a prevalent tradition that
shows—by how it treats conceptual distinctions—that it
is not rooted in experience.

Still, Gedün Chöpel undermines stances central to
much of Ge-luk-ḅa scholarship. In a lengthy section at

---

[1] *lcang skya rol pa'i rdo rje*, 1717-86.

[2] *gung thang dkon mchog bstan pa'i sgron me*, 1762-1823.

[3] *blo bzang chos kyi rgyal mtshan*, 1567?-1662.

[4] The reference is to his *Song of the Practice of the View*; see my
Meditation on Emptiness, p. 545.

the beginning of the *Ornament for the Thought of Nāgārjuna* Gedün Chöpel shows the arbitrary nature of so-called valid cognition,[1] a topic of considerable emphasis in Ge-luk-ba texts. As he says near the end of the *Treatise on Passion*:

> Examining through one's own experience how much attitudes change from childhood through to the decrepitude of old age, how could confidence be put in current conceptions! Sometimes even looking at a goddess, one is disgusted; sometimes even looking at an old woman, passion is generated. Something exists now, but later it will not be, and something else will come. Number cannot encompass the deceptions of the mind.

Also, contrary to usual Ge-luk-ba attempts to explain away the equality—for a Buddha—of a moment and an eon and the equality of a world-system and a particle by claiming that these are due to a Buddha's magical powers and thus do not contradict their mutual exclusivity, Gedün Chöpel says that the real magicians are not the Buddhas but we who through our conceptual minds make it impossible to fit a world-system in a particle and an eon in a moment. The suggestion is that Ge-luk-ba scholars would do better to orient their expositions around the enlightened perceptions of Buddhas rather than the limited perspectives of common beings.

It is a standard Ge-luk-ba posture, based on the law of the excluded middle, to refuse to accept at face value the many statements by Buddha, Nāgārjuna, and so forth that seem to deny both existence and non-existence and to explain that what they mean to refute is *inherent* existence. However, Gedün Chöpel denies the law of the

---

[1] *tshad ma, pramāṇa.* This is the part that was written in his own hand on a note pad.

excluded middle and holds that reality is indeed beyond all dualistic propositions. As he says in the *Treatise on Passion* in an interlinear note on how reality could have the seemingly contradictory qualities of emptiness and bliss:

> Regarding the inexpressible meaning that is the final nature of the stable [environment] and moving [living beings], when one considers it from a negative viewpoint it is empty and when it dawns from a positive viewpoint, it is bliss. Emptiness is a non-affirming negative, and bliss is positive, whereby one may wonder how granting the two of these to one base could be suitable, but one should not fear any reasonings that put their stock in dualistic conceptions.

His training in dialectics showed him the limits of logic.

He also criticizes literal adherence to what are actually culture-bound depictions of Pure Lands, saying that if Buddha had given the descriptions in Tibet, he would have adapted them to their culture such that Pure Lands would have wish-granting trees with leaves adorned with cups of buttered tea![1] Gedün Chöpel's attitude is not that of nihilistic relativism; he indicates not that he does not believe in Buddhahood but that Buddha spoke in accordance with what would be comprehensible to his audience. It is clear that his sharp, iconoclastic mind and wide travels gave him a sense of cultural relativism that most of his fellow Tibetans lacked.

His *Ornament for the Thought of Nāgārjuna* was so provocative that today some arch-conservative Ge-luk-bas, who cannot deny Gedün Chöpel's fame as a brilliant scholar and yet cannot imagine that anyone with intelligence could criticize Dzong-ka-ba, try to claim that the fundamental ideas found in the *Ornament for the*

---

[1] 283.8.

Thought of Nāgārjuna actually were not Gedün Chöpel's but those of his student, the Nying-ma-ba Da-wa-sang-bo.[1] The book was taken very seriously, and three refutations of it have been written: by his former teacher Shay-rap-gya-tso;[2] by Dzay-may Lo-sang-bel-den;[3] and by a fellow scholar of Go-mang College at Dre-bung, Yön-den-gya-tso.[4]

Gedün Chöpel's political opinions were also iconoclastic and got him into trouble. While he was in India, he had contacts with expatriate Tibetan political leaders, such as Rap-ga Bom-da-tsang, who had formed a political movement known as the Association for Improvement of Western Tibet.[5] The fact that Gedün

---

[1] Dren-tong Tup-den-chö-dar (*'bras mthong thub bstan chos dar*) puts forward this view in his *dge 'dun chos 'phel gyi lo rgyus*, 190-203. However, I do not accept his argument. Although I recognize that any compiler adds elements to a text, I am well aware of Tibetan attempts to rewrite history in order to serve sectarian goals. As was mentioned earlier, the publication of the text occurred before his imprisonment, and since Gedün Chöpel was an independent thinker under no one's control, the suggestion that his student and compiler Da-wa-sang-bo actually wrote the text strains credulity. Also, two of my teachers—Ge-shay Wang-gyel (*dbang rgyal*; 1901-1983) and Kensur Ngak-wang-lek-den (*mkhan zur ngag dbang legs ldan*; 1898-1971)who were contemporaries of Gedün Chöpel at Go-mang College did not question the authorship of the text. In addition, Ge-shay Gel-den did not indicate any conflict between what Gedün Chöpel told him that day in Hla-sa and what appears in the *Ornament for the Thought of Nāgārjuna*.

[2] A long unfinished work entitled *klu sgrub dgongs rgyan la che long du brtags pa mi 'jigs sengge'i nga ro*, Collected Works, vol. 3, 1-246 (Ch'inghai: mtsho sngon mi rigs dpe skrun khang, 1984).

[3] dze me blo bzang dpal ldan, *'jam dpal dgyes pa'i gtam gyi rgol gnan phye mar 'thags pa'i reg chod ral gri'i 'khrul 'khor* (Delhi: 1972).

[4] yon tan rgya mtsho, *gdong lan lung rig thog mda'* (Paris: 1977).

[5] *nub bod legs bcos kyi skyid sdug*. My translation of the name is based on Ruegg (306-307) in order to emphasize the difficulties the name itself had for the Tibetan government, described later in this paragraph. The group itself used the translation Tibet Improvement

Chöpel indicated his agreement with this progressive political movement by designing an emblem for it—a sickle, a sword, and a loom—must have particularly grated upon the more traditional and conservative members of the Tibetan government. Indeed, the very name of the organization speaks of "Western Tibet", a strange term in Tibetan that mimics the Chinese word used for Tibet, "Xizang", which literally means "western provinces". Since the term reflects the Chinese claim that the two eastern provinces of Tibet, Am-do and Kam, were already separate from Tibet, the entire movement must have been offensive to many in the Tibetan government.

The Kalimpong group published pamphlets that were critical of the Tibetan establishment, and this bothered the British administration in India which issued "quit India" notices to the group. Gedün Chöpel, after being deceitfully "invited" back to Hla-śa by a cabinet member, was taken into custody at Tso-na[1] and sent to Hla-śa where he was left on his own for some time. He brought back with him only a bed roll, a stove, a small aluminum cooking pot, and a big black metal box containing books and manuscripts. He truly had lived by the name he called himself, the "Am-do beggar".[2]

In the fall of 1947 a committee, headed by Sur-kang,[3] the most powerful person in the government in the late 1940's, condemned him ostensibly on charges of counterfeiting but actually for what were considered subversive political activities. Sur-kang subsequently accused him of being a Communist. (The rumor-mill also has

---

Party in its English language materials; the Chinese that it used in its letterheads translates as Tibet Revolutionary Party (Goldstein, 450).

[1] *mtsho sna.*

[2] This is how Stoddard's book gets its name, *Le mendiant de L'Amdo.*

[3] *zur khang dbang chen dge legs*, 1910-78.

made him a Russian spy.) More than likely, the background reasons for his arrest included his participation in the drafting of a constitution that called for parliamentary institutions (thereby challenging the aristocratic government) as well as his open religious iconoclasm. Also, the Tibetan government feared the Guomindang backing of the Association for Improvement of Western Tibet. Gedün Chöpel himself later explained that he thought the British government plotted to have him arrested as a Communist because of his historical research showing Tibet to be an independent nation whose boundaries extended into India, whereas the British recognized Chinese suzerainty over Tibet and wanted to maintain the borders of their empire.

When the authorities came to arrest him, he made two requests—(1) that they not disturb the myriad of notes he had made on pieces of paper and cigarette wrappers carefully arranged around his room since they were a draft of a book proving the independent status of the Tibetan nation and (2) that they keep secret the fact that, to take care of his sexual needs without the drain on his time that a wife would be, he kept a life-size rubber woman (that he had painted with the face of a nomad). In time, neither of these requests was honored.

The Cabinet insisted on seeing all of his writings, and since none of them incriminated him, they interrogated him, eventually resorting to flogging. Gedün Chöpel denied all. Despite the lack of substantial evidence, he was jailed with common criminals. In prison he spent his nights with an illiterate woman of Avaho origin.

In 1949 Rahula Sankrityayana and George Roerich met with Sur-kang's brother, a general, while he was visiting India; they urged him to put Gedün Chöpel to the task of writing a history of Tibet and told him that better treatment of him would bring benefit to Tibet. They told him that Gedün Chöpel's friendship with

China could profitably be used by the Tibetan government when the inevitable take-over by the Communist
Chinese occurred. After two years and four months of
imprisonment, he emerged in 1949,[1] unkempt, very
thin, and dressed in smelly rags.

The treatment he received is particularly poignant in
the light of the stanzas found at the end of the *Treatise
on Passion*, where he insists that others' faults not be im-
puted to him:

> Do not put on a humble person's head
> One's own individual faults, like the destruction
> Of the lifestyle of friends with proper behavior
> Or the loss of composure of the pretentious, and
> so forth.

He makes the wish that humble beings have freedom
from persecution:

> May all the humble who act on this broad earth
> Have manifest freedom from the pit of merciless
> laws,
> And in common be able to partake of small plea-
> sures,
> Necessary and suitable, with independence.

This stanza expresses what has become the plight of the
Tibetan people—the aspirations of people denied human rights under cruel domination.

The government seal on his cell was broken by Liu-
shar Tup-den-tar-ba,[2] the head of the Department of
External Security Affairs, to whom his request for release had been referred. The fifteen-year-old Dalai

---

[1] K. Dhondup says it was November, 1950.

[2] *leu* (or *sne 'u*) *shar thub bstan thar pa*, died mid-1980's. I came to
know Liu-shar well at the Lamaist Buddhist Monastery of America
where he stayed for a few years before being called back to India by
the Dalai Lama, but I do not remember our discussing Gedün
Chöpel.

Lama, who had recently assumed the reins of government, granted a general amnesty to free all prisoners, and this brought Liu-shar to Gedün Chöpel's cell-door. Inside, he found walls lined with cobwebs and his few possessions infested with worms; Liu-shar felt he had arrived in the dwelling-place of Tibet's most famous ascetic Mi-la-re-ba.[1] On the wall was a stanza that poignantly captures the plight of the prisoner:[2]

> From the sphere of compassion may those with
>   the eye of wisdom take heed
> Of an honest small child left alone
> In the dense forest where a stubborn tiger
> Mad with the blood of jealousy so frighteningly
>   roars.

The "tiger" is the Regent Dak-drak,[3] the first syllable of whose name means tiger. Gedün Chöpel blamed him for his imprisonment.

He emerged from prison unkempt and in rags. He had become an alcoholic chain-smoking opium addict. His large black metal box of manuscripts and books was nowhere to be seen.

For two and half months he refused to clean up, dress in clean clothes, shave, or cut his hair which reached to his waist. He described himself as a precious lapis lazuli vase that had been broken against stone. Though his life never came back together, he nevertheless demonstrated his still considerable abilities in debate with five scholars from Dre-bung who came to visit him, but only after throwing ash and blowing cigarette smoke on a painting of Shākyamuni Buddha to the appalled amazement of his visitors. The debate revolved around whether a Buddha has actual feeling of pleasure and

---

[1] *mi la ras pa.*

[2] La-chung-a-po, 651.2.

[3] *stag brag.*

pain; the five of them together could not defeat him and left in silence. It is reported that afterwards one of them was so impressed by Gedün Chöpel's arguments that he was depressed over his own lack of knowledge. On another occasion over beer Gedün Chöpel demonstrated his knowledge of about thirteen languages—those mentioned above as well as Japanese, Hindi, Bhutanese, Nepali, Sikkimese, and so forth. The government gave him a pension and rations, but his black box of manuscripts and books was never returned. Some think it was sent to the British.

For two months after being released from prison Gedün Chöpel lived together with the illiterate nomad that he had met in prison. He sent her back to her homeland after having a friend buy for her whatever she wanted. Later, he lived with a woman from Chamdo[1] by the name of Yu-drön.[2]

His health weakened from heavy drinking and smoking. The Dalai Lama's personal physician prescribed medicines but to no avail. Two years after his release from prison, listening to Dzong-ka-ba's *Praise of Dependent-Arising*[3] and Mi-pam's *Prayer-Wishes for the Basis, Path, and Fruit of the Great Completeness*,[4] he announced, "Those were nice to hear. Mad Gedün Chöpel has seen all of the intriguing sights of this world. Now,

---

[1] *chab mdo.*

[2] *g.yu sgron.*

[3] The full title is *Praise of the Supramundane Victor Buddha from the Approach of His Teaching the Profound Dependent-Arising, The Essence of the Good Explanations* (*rten 'brel bstod pa/sangs rgyas bcom ldan 'das la zab mo rten cing 'brel bar 'byung ba gsung ba'i sgo nas bstod pa legs par bshad pa'i snying po*), P6016, vol. 153. For an English translation, see Geshe Wangyal, *The Door of Liberation* (New York: Lotsawa, 1978), pp. 117-25; also: Robert Thurman, *Life and Teachings of Tsong Khapa* (Dharamsala: Library of Tibetan Works and Archives, 1982), pp. 99-107.

[4] *rdzogs chen gyi gzhi lam 'bras bu'i smon lam.*

having heard that there is a famous land down below, I wonder what it would be like if I went to look." He was wryly suggesting that he was about to go to a hell. The sun was setting; so, he suggested his close friend (and biographer) La-chung-a-po leave and look in on him the next day. When La-chung-a-po returned, he was told that Gedün Chöpel passed away soon after he left.

The years in prison had left their mark. He died in 1951 at age forty-six, a shadow of his former self.

2 Sources for the Treatise on Passion

Gedün Chöpel finished the *Treatise on Passion* during an active and productive period of his life in mid-winter of 1938 in Mathurā, India. The sources that he used are in four classes:

1 Indian texts
2 Tibetan texts
3 An Indian informant
4 His own experience.

Indian texts. At the end of the book he indicates that the composition has its roots in Indian erotic literature:

> The root of the explication runs back to Indian texts.
> The verse was put together in the Tibetan style, easy to understand.
> Hence I have the feeling that from the cause of its not being incomplete
> It will definitely give rise to wonderful effects.

In recognition of his primary sources, he pays homage

in the opening section to Hindu deities Maheshvara and Gaurī:

> Obeisance to the feet of Maheshvara
> Whose appealing body has the cast of the stainless sky,
> Who eternally plays in the glory of pleasure without emission,
> And who resides on the snowy Mount Kailāsa of Tibet.

> I bow down to the feet of the goddess Gaurī,[1]
> Whose beautiful face has the cast of the full moon,
> Whose smiling white teeth are like a pearl rosary,
> Whose swelling breasts have the form of a bulbous conch.

Gedün Chöpel mentions that there are over thirty Indian texts, large and small, on the topic of sex. Of these, he lists eight:[2]

- *Sūtra on Passion (kāmasūtra)*[3] by Mallanāga Vātsyāyana. This is the famous *Kāma Sūtra* written in the third century. According to Hindu tradition, Brahmā uttered 100,000 chapters on Dharma (religious duty), Artha (wealth), and Kāma (passion). Nandī is said to have collected together the one thousand chapters on passion. Shvetaketu, son of Uddālaka, condensed Nandī's work into five hundred chapters, and Bābhravya, an inhabitant of the Punjab, condensed Shvetaketu's text into seven sections with one hundred fifty chapters. The seven sections were

---

[1] She is also known as Durgā and Pārvatī.

[2] Listed in chronological order.

[3] *'dod pa'i mdo*. For translations, see the Bibliography. The thirteenth-century commentary by Yashodhara, the *Jayamaṅgalā*, is usually published along with the Sanskrit text.

supplemented and summarized by seven scholars in separate treatises, the section on sexual union being done by Suvarṇanābha. Mallanāga Vātsyāyana, a Kashmiri Brahmin from Kishtawar District, retained Bābhravya's format of seven sections and, using the various expositions, constructed a new text called the *Kāma Sūtra*.[1] From among these, only the *Kāma Sūtra* survives.[2]

* *Secrets of Sexual Pleasure (ratirahasya)*[3] by Kokkoka. Written in the ninth or tenth century,[4] this book is also known as the *Kokashāstra* after its author. Kokkoka relies on Nandikeshvara, Goṇikaputra, and Vātsyāyana as well as at least a dozen others. In India the *Ratirahasya* is second in popularity only to the *Kāma Sūtra* and was translated into Persian. The principal commentary is by Kāñchīnātha.

---

[1] For this history, see *Kāma Sūtra*, I.1.

[2] For a helpful book on pre-*Kāma Sūtra* erotics in India, see P. K. Agrawala, *The Unknown Kamasutras* (Varanasi: Books Asia, 1983).

[3] *dga'i ba'i gsang ba*. For a Sanskrit edition with Kāñcinātha's commentary see Kokkoka, *Ratirahasya*, ed. D. Parajuli (Lahore: n.d.). For English translations with introductions see Alex Comfort, *The Koka Shastra, Being the Ratirahasya of Kokkoka, and Other Medieval Indian Writings on Love* (London: George Allen and Unwin, 1964); and S. C. Upadhyaya, *Kokashastra (Rati Rahasya) of Pandit Kokkoka* (Bombay: Taraporevala, 1965). There are three other commentaries on the *Ratirahasya*—by "Avancha Rama Chandra, Kavi Prabhu, and Harihara" (P. Thomas, 76).

  Rati is the spouse of the Love-God, and thus *Ratirahasya* also means "Secrets of Rati".

[4] Moti Chandra (54) gives the limits of Kokkoka's dates as in the ninth or tenth centuries, though impossible to fix precisely. Alex Comfort (46) reports that Pisani dates him in the twelfth century and Lienhard, in the eleventh or twelfth.

  Gedün Chöpel reports that parts of an Indian edition of Kokkoka's text are to be found in Ngor Monastery, which is located in Dzang Province (*gtsang*), near Shi-ḡa-dzay (*gzhi ka rtse*).

- *Arts of Passion (kāmakalā).*[1] Perhaps this is the *Kalāvilāsa* by the eleventh-century Kashmiri Kshemendra.[2]

- *Treatise on Desire (rāgaśāstra?)*[3] by Maheshvara. This text is a mystery, but it may be the *Rāgashekhara* that is ascribed to Jyotirīshvara[4] (first half of the fourteenth century). Since it is reported[5] that Jyotirīshvara condensed works on erotics, including one by Īshvara, to create his *Collection of Five Arrows*, it may be that the *Rāgashekhara* was composed not by Jyotirīshvara but by another author of the name Īshvara, i.e., Maheshvara.[6] Gedün Chöpel declares that the *Treatise on Desire* by Maheshvara and the *Kāma Sūtra* by Vātsyāyana are the best, and thus it is mysterious that the former does not appear to have been available to Indian scholars of eroticism in this century.[7]

---

[1] *'dod pa'i sgyu rtsal.*

[2] See Moti Chandra, 57. For a Sanskrit edition see Kṣemendra, *Kalāvilāsa*, Kāvyamāla, ed. 1888. For a German translation see R. Schmidt (Leipzig: 1914).

[3] *chags pa'i bstan bcos.*

[4] Bhattacharya, 115. He cites "Chakrabarti in *JASB* [*Journal of the Anthropological Society of Bombay*], 1915, p. 414", but the citation is inaccurate.

[5] Moti Chandra, 59.

[6] Bhattacharya (110) reports that sometime between the tenth and fourteenth centuries the Buddhist Padmashrī used a text by Maheshvara in the composition of his *Nāgarasarvasva*, but that nothing is known about Maheshvara or his text. Could the text be the *Rāgashekhara*?

The Sanskrit of the *Nāgarasarvasva* with Jagajjyotirmall's commentary has been edited by Tansukhram Sharma (Bombay: M. I. Desai Pub., 1921). According to Comfort (98), some think that Padmashrī was a monk while others think Padmashrī was a woman.

[7] Another possibility is that Maheshvara is Nandikeshvara who figures prominently in Kokkoka's *Ratirahasya*, in which case Maheshvara's *Treatise on Desire (chags pa'i bstan bcos, rāgaśāstra?)* would be the *Ratirahasya* itself since it seeks specifically to include

- *Collection of Five Arrows (pañcasāyaka),*[1] by Jyotirīsha, i.e., Maithila Jyotirīshvara Kavishekhara. Written in the first half of the fourteenth century,[2] the book is divided into five chapters, or five flower-headed arrows of the God of Love.

- *Jeweled Lamp of Sexual Pleasure (ratiratnapradīpikā)*[3] by Devarāja, written in the fifteenth century.[4]

- *Form of the Bodiless One (anaṅgaranga),*[5] by King Kalyāṇamalla. The Bodiless One is the god of desire, Kāma. Based on the *Kāma Sūtra* and the *Ratirahasya*, this text was written early in the sixteenth century to please Ladakhan, son of King Ahmada of the Lodi dynasty.[6] Through Muslim patronage the work was widely circulated, having been freely translated into

---

Nandikeshvara's views. That this is not entirely farfetched is suggested by the fact that Gedün Chöpel begins his presentation with a fourfold depiction of types of females which he says is drawn from Maheshvara's text and which is found at the beginning of the *Ratirahasya* explicitly drawn from Nandikeshvara and Goṇikāputra. Counter-evidence is that Gedün Chöpel also gives a fourfold classification of males, whereas the *Ratirahasya* repeats Vātsyāyana's threefold classification. In short, the *chags pa'i bstan bcos* is a mystery.

[1] *mda' lnga pa.* For a Sanskrit edition, see Jyotirīshvara, *Pañcasāyaka,* ed. S. Shastri Ghiladia (Lahore: 1921).

[2] Moti Chandra, 59. Richard Schmidt dates it in the fourteenth century (Comfort, 82).

[3] *dga'i ba'i rin chen rnam gsal.* See Devarāja, *Ratiratnapradīpikā,* ed. with English translation by K. Rangaswami Iyengar (Mysore: 1923).

[4] Moti Chandra, 60.

[5] *lus med yan lag;* the Tibetan could be translated as *Limb of the Bodiless [One].* For the Sanskrit text, see Kalyāṇamalla, *Anaṅgaranga,* ed. R. Shastri Kusala (Lahore: 1890). For English translations, see Sir Richard Burton and F. F. Arbuthnot, *The Ananga Ranga or the Hindu Art of Love of Kalyana Malla* (London: 1885; New York: G. P. Putnam's Sons, 1964); also, T. L. Ray, *Ananga-Ranga* (Calcutta: Medical Book Agency, 1960).

[6] Moti Chandra, 61.

Urdu, Persian, and Arabic by Muslim writers.[1] In India it is third in popularity after the *Kāma Sūtra* and the *Ratirahasya*.

- *Crest Jewel of the God of Passion (kandarpacūḍāmaṇi),*[2] said to be by King Vīrabhadra but probably by a court poet. Written around 1577,[3] it is a transposition of the *Kāma Sūtra* into verse.

Gedün Chöpel mentions two other texts:

- A treatise by Nāgārjuna. Gedün Chöpel indicates that he only heard that there is such a text. This may be the *Treatise on Sexual Pleasure (ratiśāstra)*[4] attributed to Nāgārjuna Siddha. The work is placed anywhere from the seventh to the tenth century.[5] It deals with astrology, prenatal influences, and so forth.[6]

- *Brief Treatise on Passion* by Surūpa.[7] This short text is found in the tantra section of the Translation of the

---

[1] P. Thomas, 76. It was also translated into Turkish (Burton, 14).

[2] *'dod lha'i gtsug nor*. For a Sanskrit edition see Virabhadra, *Kandarpacuḍāmaṇi*, ed. by R. Sastri Kusala (Lahore: 1926).

[3] Bhattacharya, 122.

[4] Also called *ratiśāstraratnāvalī*. For the text, see Richard Schmidt, "Das Ratiśāstra des Nāgārjuna" in *Wiener Zeitschrift für die Kunde des Morgenlandes*, XXIII, 1909, pp. 180-183. For a translation into English, see Nāgārjuna Siddha, *Ratiśāstra*, translated by A. C. Ghose (Calcutta: Seal, 1904). Kokkoka's *Ratirahasya* contains five recipes from Nāgārjuna for hypnotizing a person, delaying ejaculation, female orgasm, impregnation, and painless delivery; see S. C. Upadhyaya, *Kokashāstra*, 100-101.

[5] S. C. Upadhyaya, *Kokashāstra*, 7.

[6] Comfort, 99.

[7] *gzugs bzang zhabs*. The Sanskrit of his name is not given in the colophon of the work, but the compilers of the *Tibetan Tripiṭaka* (Tokyo-Kyoto: Tibetan Tripiṭaka Research Foundation, 1956) speculate that it is Surūpa. It might also be Abhirūpapāda. I have not found any reference to either name in Indian erotic literature.

Treatises.[1] Nothing appears to be known about its author. At the beginning of the text, he says that he is drawing from Nāgārjuna's condensation of the vast science of erotics.

Gedün Chöpel concludes his discussion of Indian sources by saying:

> Putting together the large and the small, there are over thirty. The best among them are the *Treatise on Desire* by Maheshvara and the *Sūtra on Passion* by Vātsyāyana. Here I will explicate the arts of passion in reliance on those.

It is unclear whether the word "those"[2] refers just to the texts by Maheshvara and Vātsyāyana or also to the others. Until a study of Maheshvara's text is done, it is cannot be determined that Gedün Chöpel necessarily took Indian material—that is not in Vātsyāyana's *Sūtra on Passion* but is, for instance, in Kokkoka's *Secrets of Pleasure*—from the latter, since Maheshvara may have drawn from Kokkoka. However, the difficulties of finding Maheshvara's text appear to be insuperable.

It is clear, nevertheless, that Gedün Chöpel did not just translate Indian materials into Tibetan. He used Indian texts as general sources for elaboration from his own creativity.

Tibetan texts. Gedün Chöpel asks readers to compare his book written from experience to another by the monk Ju Mi-pam-gya-tso[3] (1846-1912), which he says was written not from experience but only from scholarly study.

> The venerable Mi-pam wrote from having studied [these topics],

---

[1] *bstan 'gyur*; P3323, vol. 157, 31.5.2-33.1.1.

[2] *de.* The singular is often used for the plural.

[3] *'ju mi pham rgya mtsho/mi pham 'jam dbyangs rnam rgyal.*

And the lascivious Chöpel wrote from experience.
That these two [treatises] differ in terms of their
impact will be known
By passionate males and females through putting
them into practice.

Thus, it is clear that he was familiar with Mi-pam's
*Treatise on Passion: Treasure Thoroughly Pleasing the
World,*[1] a text about a third the length of Gedün
Chöpel's and more difficult stylistically.

When asked who was more wise, Mi-pam or Dzong-
ka-ba, Gedün Chöpel responded that if they debated,
Dzong-ka-ba would win because he was more profi-
cient in debate but that in terms of basic knowledge and
capacities in exposition Mi-pam was stronger.[2] Still, it is
clear that Gedün Chöpel felt that on the topic of sex, he
knew a good deal more than Mi-pam.

Though both texts begin with descriptions of types of
males and females, Mi-pam quickly proceeds to describe
the sixty-four arts of love after brief advice on prepara-
tions. Gedün Chöpel, on the other hand, adds material
on facial marks and their meaning as well as stages of
life, and then sets the scene with four chapters on (1) the
importance of sex and the plight of women in a male-
dominated world; (2) how to prepare the vagina for
penetration, the meaning of the time of the first menstruation, and the right age for starting sex; (3) an exposition on essential fluids in the male and female bodies, the physical similarities of male and female, and the
gradual but deeper passion of females; (4) and a report
on the sexual habits of women from various parts of
India.

---

[1] *'dod pa'i bstan bcos 'jig rten kun tu dga' ba'i gter.* Published in the
back of the 1969 and 1983 editions of Gedün Chöpel's work, 103-
137.

[2] La-chung-a-po, 649.2-649.9.

With regard to the sixty-four arts, Gedün Chöpel's descriptions are more expansive, containing titillating detail and often differing even in the names of the individual arts from Mi-pam. For instance, on the eight embraces Gedün Chöpel's exposition is twice as long as Mi-pam's, and whereas Mi-pam offers only five lines on the eight kisses, Gedün Chöpel gives two and half pages along with advice on where and when to kiss in accordance with an Indian theory of the movement of an inner essential fluid in the body during the lunar month. On pinching and scratching Mi-pam has a page, whereas Gedün Chöpel has two and half that contextualize the act. Before passing on to postures of copulation, Gedün Chöpel inserts two chapters of advice on how to enhance the intensity of pleasure that are often lyric in their appealing beauty. For instance:

> Seeing the arrow of passion not drawn on the
>   bow of flowers,
> The jewel[1] filled with the milk of ambrosia,
> And that with the oily red color of coral,
> Even the daughters of the gods will fall to the
>   ground.

> Merely touching with the tip of the jewel is the
>   taste.
> Entering is the delicious molasses itself.
> Rubbing and pressing are the sweet honey.
> Give to me the various delicious sweet tastes.

Mi-pam's text is dry by comparison.

Gedün Chöpel's chapter on "Playing with the Organ" is similarly replete with appealing descriptions of the female's playing with the male organ, written from the viewpoint of the female. Also, his chapter on postures of copulation itself begins with a long discussion of passion and the need to arouse the female before doing the

---

[1] Head of the phallus.

deed; then he describes with luscious detail not just eight postures but also twelve others. Mi-pam, on the other hand, lists the eight postures with minimal description in less than a page.

With regard to the eight postures of role reversal the two texts offer different lists. Gedün Chöpel then pro - ceeds to give eight more postures of copulation to complete the count of sixty-four, whereas Mi-pam stops at fifty-six despite speaking as if there were sixty-four.

In the remaining twenty pages of his text[1] Mi-pam writes on topics of tantric sexual yoga that are not in Gedün Chöpel's book. These include mantras, visualizations, and potions to improve sexual performance and pleasure; gazes; a large number of postures including ones associated with gods, demi-gods, humans, and animals (nāgas); and potions for non-emission when visualization and meditation are not successful. He also mentions that there are profound mantras, visualizations, and potions to be used during the stage of completion in Highest Yoga Tantra that are to be obtained from a competent lama.[2]

As will be detailed below in Chapter Five, Gedün Chöpel chose not to include in his text such specifically tantric and thus secret material on potions and so forth intended for persons of high yogic ability even though the tantric doctrine of the fundamental innate mind of clear light underlies much of his presentation. His intention was to present a text on sexual arts that, while imbedded in tantric perspectives, does not contravene dictums of secrecy. In terms of the intimate, vivid, and enticing detail that he provides on the sexual arts, his

---

[1] 116-137, which is over half of his short text.

[2] At the end of his text Mi-pam indicates that his sources include Surūpa's condensation of Nāgārjuna's text which itself, he says, is a condensation of the *Kāmashāstra* by "Sva-ra-a-ni". Most likely, he used Surūpa's text as one of his sources for the latter part of his exposition that I have outlined in this paragraph.

claim to have exceeded Mi-pam is indeed well-founded. With regard to other Tibetan material, Gedün Chöpel must have been familiar with the love poems of the Sixth Dalai Lama. He also would have heard many of the rascally tales of the infamous Uncle Dön-ba,[1] such as when he puts on a nun's habit and goes to stay for several months in a nunnery with the result that many nuns become pregnant. Uncle Dön-ba gets away with his ruse for a while but eventually is caught and bound as punishment though he escapes through guile much like Brer Rabbit.

An Indian informant. Gedün Chöpel mentions that "The explicator of difficult passages was an old Brahmin." The Brahmin must have been a Sanskrit scholar familiar with Indian erotic literature; he helped with difficult passages in Sanskrit texts mentioned above.

His own experience. Since Gedün Chöpel was a monk, the question of whether he actually had sexual contacts naturally arises. The *Treatise on Passion* offers copious evidence that he did. First, he speaks of his devotion to the topic of erotics when, in the section on whether women have a regenerative emission, he says:

> Because I like conversation about the lower parts, I asked many women friends, but aside from shaking a fist at me with shame and laughter, I could not find even one who would give an honest answer.

He speaks of his long-standing attraction to women and that his vows of celibacy contradicted this:

---

[1] *a khu ston pa.* See *Tales of Uncle Tompa, The Legendary Rascal of Tibet*, compiled and translated by Rinjing Dorje (San Rafael, California: Dorje Ling, 1975). K. Dhondup (13) also mentions the *"Khok-buk"* of Day-si Šang-gyay-gya-tso (*sde srid sangs rgyas rgya mtsho*) as a medical forerunner of Gedün Chöpel's text.

I have little shame and great faith in women.
From the past I indeed have not had a head for
vows, the type who binds the bad and casts aside
the good, but recently the entrails [i.e., even the
remnants] of deception have ceased here [in
India].

He suggests that previously when he kept his vows of
monkhood, he was involved in self-deception, which
ended when he relinquished them in India.

More explicitly, he indicates that due to his expertise
in sex it became his lot to write a book about the topic
for Tibetans:

The acquaintance of a watery fish is profound
   when it comes to water.
One has more knowledge of what one has expe-
   rienced.
Thinking this, I wrote with hard work
This treatise that is my lot.

Specifically, after detailing the sexual habits of areas
within India, he declares that he has had sexual contact
with women from two of Tibet's provinces, Kam[1] and
Dzang.[2] He says that given his lack of experience with
the three other areas of Tibet, he would not pretend to
write about Tibetan women in any detail:

These natures of women should be explained
through associating them also with the country
of Tibet, but because I have had acquaintance
with none other than women of Kam and Dzang,
I do not have detailed understanding. The
women of Kam have soft flesh and are very affectionate. The women of Dzang are skilled in
technique; they are good at moving about

---

[1] *khams.*

[2] *gtsang.*

beneath a man.

This little outline of the women of Tibet was written for the sake of calling other passionate persons to the task. Here the methods of lying, moving, and so forth of the women of Am-do, Kam, Central Tibet, Dzang, and Ñga-ri[1] could be added by a knowledgeable old man who has experienced the world.

Hence, from his own words, we know that he had sexual contacts with women from the southeastern province of Kam and the western province of Dzang. Since he finished writing this book in 1938 in India, one can only wonder whether these contacts took place in Tibet or occurred with Tibetan women who were living or traveling in India.

Gedün Chöpel's sexual experience also included Indian women. He identifies a "Kashmiri girl" as having given "naked instruction[2] in experience". The term "naked instruction" is usually used in a religious context to refer a type of discourse in which "the words of a text are explained in terms of what they actually refer to, not merely in terms of their literal meaning."[3] Gedün Chöpel amusingly uses this term for a type of religious instruction to describe a girl's instructing him in sexual practices. The pun exhibits his playfulness and also reflects the culture's perspective that the spheres of religion and of sex are not separate.

Gedün Chöpel similarly uses vocabulary usually limited to religious texts to indicate his depth of knowledge about sex:

This *Treatise on Passion* was written by Gedün

---

[1] *mnga' ris.*

[2] *dmar khrid.*

[3] See Gedün Lodrö, *Walking Through Walls: A Presentation of Tibetan Meditation* (Ithaca: Snow Lion Publications, 1992).

> Chöpel who passed to the far side of our own
> [Buddhist] and others' [non-Buddhist] topics of
> knowledge, like an ocean, and who eliminated
> false superimpositions with regard to sexual de-
> sire through seeing, hearing, and experiencing.

He uses the religious vocabulary of passing to the other
side of the ocean of Buddhist and non-Buddhist fields of
knowledge but modifies the standard religious process
of removing ignorance through the trilogy of hearing,
thinking, and meditating to removing wrong ideas
about sexual desire through "seeing, hearing, and experiencing". The usage of vocabulary usually confined
to the sacred sphere for knowledge of sexual arts is at
once amusing and scandalous. Like many actions during
his life, on the surface it suggests a lack of faith in
Buddhism but actually pokes fun at false distinctions between religious and worldly life.

Even more specifically, he identifies by name one
Tibetan and two Indian women with whom he experienced sexual relations:

> May the girls who have physical connection with
>   me—
> Yu-drön, Gangā, Asali, and so forth—
> Pass along the path from pleasure to pleasure
> And arrive at the place of the Truth Body[1] of
>   great bliss.

The Tibetan woman, Yu-drön, is said not to be the
woman by the same name with whom he lived near the
end of his life. Gangā, most likely, is the woman in
whose house he finished the *Treatise on Passion* in
Mathurā. At the end of the book he refers to her as
"Gangā Deva from Pañcāla, girl-friend with the same
life-style". That she had the same life-style probably

---

[1] *chos sku, dharmakāya*. One of the endowments of Buddhahood.

means that she shared his avid interest in the lower parts.

From this evidence, internal to his text, it is clear that despite having once been a monk with vows of celibacy, he wrote the *Treatise on Passion* from experience with Tibetan and Indian women.

3 Equality of Women

Gedün Chöpel's text is, for the most part, built around an exposition of the sixty-four arts of love. Although a number of recurrent themes are woven into the material, these are often so widely interspersed and the author so abruptly switches both tone and subject that points can be missed in the colliding juxtapositions of the collage. In one sense, these shifts are part of the charm of the text, the voice of earlier themes intruding at sometimes unexpected points into the exposition; however, the shifts are often so abrupt that the mind does not dwell on topics worthy of consideration but is drawn into a new subject. I am reminded of the book on Tibetan independence that Gedün Chöpel had written on hundreds of scraps of paper arranged around his room in Hla-śa. Similarly, although the *Treatise on Passion* is a finished work, its fragmentary treatment of subjects makes it likely that dominant themes will remain hidden, and thus I will bring together the scattered parts on central themes so that their impact will not be missed.

49

In addition to the sixty-four arts of love, the *Treatise on Passion* has at least six recurrent themes:

* the equality of women
* sexual pleasure and spiritual insight
* an ethic of love
* techniques for increasing female sexual pleasure
* advice on pregnancy
* classificatory schemes.

EQUALITY OF WOMEN

Repeatedly, Gedün Chöpel shows sensitivity for the plight of women victimized by social customs and legal codes. About adultery he says:

> There is no difference between men and women with regard to adultery. If one examines it carefully, men are worse. A king's having a thousand queens is still proclaimed as high-class style. If a woman has a hundred men, she is slandered as if there is nothing comparable.

He complains that wealth and position buy men not only immunity for their acts but also praise for what is actually a fault.

Although women are derided for instability of character, whatever instability they have is due to how they are treated in a man's world:

> If [a king] does it alternately with a thousand women, where is there any sense of adultery! Since doing it with a wife is not adultery, how could the rich ever be adulterous! An old man of wealth with hair like snow selects and buys a young girl. Being a mere article sold, she is given a price. Alas, women have no protectors! When a man chooses and takes her by force, the woman has not come to him by her own wish; therefore,

like trying to patch wood with stone, how could the natures of women be stable!

He mocks customs built on a double standard:

In Nepal even if a man takes a woman forcibly and acts out his passion, when he finishes she rises, touches her head to his feet, and goes. First, she struggles, saying, "No," and afterwards bows saying, "Thank you." Thinking about it, one bursts out laughing; it is even said those who do so have good behavior.

He derides the institutionalization of misogyny as well as fawning acquiescence that results in lack of political action:

In the country of Persia[1] each old man takes about ten young wives, but if one wife commits adultery, she is immediately killed by being burned alive. Though one man is satisfied with five young women, how could five young women be satisfied with one old man? In that way, in many areas of the world the wealthy have many laws and customs of their own wish. This is given the name of goodness, and since it meets with the wishes of the king of the country, the skillful also show smiling approval. If one thinks about it, there is no relief from sorrow. So, do not listen just to the great noise proclaimed in one voice by beings of the same male sex; for once, witness the characteristics of the truth and speak only the honest speech of the unbiased!

Gedün Chöpel rouses his readers to social action.

He describes the world as an abode of suffering buffeted by the effects of actions (*karma*) committed earlier in this lifetime and in other lifetimes and says that when

---

[1] *ta zig.*

life is seen as such a desert of pain, the value of a companion who is like a goddess, a field, a nurse, a poet, a servant, and a friend can be appreciated:

> This huge world is like a great fearful desert; by the power of many former actions beings definitely will suffer. That which is able to bestow the comforts of pleasure in such a world seems to be the magic of the deeds of a playful woman-friend. She is the goddess with a body which when seen brings pleasure. She is the field producing a good family lineage. She is the mother acting as a nurse when one is sick and a poet consoling the mind when one is sad. She is a servant who does all of the work of the household. She is a friend who protects with fun and joy for a lifetime. One's wife with whom one has become related through former actions (*karma*) is endowed with these six qualities. Hence, the claim that women are unstable and adulterous is extremely untrue.

He mocks customs that allow men to be adulterous but treat women who do the same as unfit for association:

> Some men keep a mistress and then give her up. It is said that the pure gods fear to be touched even by a breeze that has scattered the dust of the feet of a woman of degenerate body and ethics; it is said the gods will run away.

He blames such customs on non-Buddhist views that do not recognize the basic nature of suffering and thereby discriminate some as clean and some as dirty:

> The insides of the body are all only dirty; outside all beings have skin.[1] The discrimination of hu-

---

[1] Nāgārjuna's *Precious Garland* (stanzas 148-166), with which Gedün Chöpel would have been familiar, voices the same opinion, but in

mans into clean and dirty has its source in non-Buddhist systems.

From a Buddhist viewpoint, the body is a product molded by actions in former lifetimes that are driven by ignorance, and thus the coarse body of flesh, blood, and bone is simply not clean.

Gedün Chöpel blames various prohibitions on the selfishness of Brahmin clerics:

> It is said in some systems of behavior that because widows are unclean, food made by them should not be eaten; however, this is a transmission of the speech of compassionless Brahmins. In ancient times in India, a woman, when her husband died, would die by jumping onto the pyre. If she could not jump onto the fire, she was considered to be a living corpse; the source of a widow's uncleanliness is only that.

And:

> The followers of the master Bābhravya say that there is no fault in doing it with another's wife if she is not the wife of a Brahmin or a Guru. This is deception with shameless lies; as most authors of tracts used to be Brahmins, they wrote this way. If an intelligent person challenges the presentations in such deceitful tracts with scriptural quotes, [the truth] will be known. It is clearly said

---

the next stanza he says:
  Whoever composes poetry with
  Metaphors which elevate this body--
  O how shameless! O how stupid!
  How embarrassing before the wise!

See Nāgārjuna and the Seventh Dalai Lama, *The Precious Garland and the Song of the Four Mindfulnesses* (New York: Harper and Row, 1975); reprinted in *The Buddhism of Tibet* (London: George Allen and Unwin, 1983, and Ithaca: Snow Lion Publications, 1987).

in the *Kālachakra Tantra* that Brahmins have a black disposition for their wives.

He takes a relativistic view on customs that prohibit relations with widows:

Though much has been said about the features that make women fit and unfit for the act,[1] it is mostly sufficient to proceed according to the customs prevalent in one's own area. Indians are strongly prohibited and constrained from copulating with a widow. When this is examined with reasoning, one sees no prohibition and even sees great benefit [in having sexual relations with widows]. Therefore, widows who have finished their grief and are young are suitable for the deed.

He extends this openness to relatives but strictly prohibits adultery:

Moreover, there are many explanations that relatives of the same lineage and so forth are not suitable partners, but other than only being customs of individual areas, it is difficult to determine in one point what is suitable and what is not. However, copulation with another's wife is a basis for the breaking of friendship and the arising of fights and controversy. As this is a bad, shameless deed bringing suffering in this and future lives, good people should avoid it like a contagious disease.

The standard Buddhist view on adultery is that it brings discord in this life (when the other's mate finds out) and establishes a karmic base such that in a future life one will be faced with discord and with difficulty in finding a suitable mate.

---

[1] See, for instance, *Kāma Sūtra* I.5.

On these practical grounds, Gedün Chöpel disagrees with the view that it is suitable to sleep with someone whose mate is far away:

> It is explained in the *Kāma Sūtra* that it is suitable to do it with the wife of a man who has gone far away, but since the birth of a child in the not distant future brings problems like those mentioned above, it is best to avoid this.

Instead of treating women this way, he recommends a relativistic perspective:

> There are many countries where uncles and nieces live together, where brother and sister live together, or brothers and sisters of the same father live together. That country where there is a society agreeing with one's own lineage has good customs.

However, this is not relativism that could be used to justify mistreatment of women as a local custom; rather, he recommends a moral stance founded in the equality of the sexes. Calling for recognition that a couple is a single unit, he says:

> Half of the body of a husband is his wife, and half of the body of a wife is her husband. With one's body split in half, it is difficult even to enter among animals. Thinking so, if one can reach the end of the lifetime having established a mind of love toward one's mate without being two-faced, even one's corpse will be an object of worship.

He holds that success in the inter-personal relationship of marriage—a worldly matter in Buddhism—is karmically so good that, like Buddhist saints, one's corpse should be put in a reliquary and become an object of worship. Again, his conflation of the secular and the religious is iconoclastically scandalous in Tibetan society.

However, he is indicating that the ground for cultivating basic religious attitudes such as love and compassion is right in the home. In order to establish the equality of males and females, Gedün Chöpel even dispels the notion that the two sexes are so different physically. After explaining that certain differences are merely due to a female's being subject to menstruation, he details intriguing physical correspondences between the sexes:

> Because a woman menstruates, her physical power is less, her flesh is soft and loose, her skin is thin, her feeling is extremely sharp, and when old, she has many wrinkles. However, there are no differences in the bodies of male and female by way of external shape. Among whatever a male has, there is nothing a female does not have; even the penis and gonads are inside the female genitalia. The skin of the male collected at the root of his organ are the labia on the sides of the vagina. Underneath the labia is a small bit of flesh, about the size of a finger [the clitoris]; when passion is produced, it rises and becomes hard. It is the equivalent of the male member, and if it is tickled with a finger, passion is quickly produced in women. At the time of copulation the clitoris is so, and moreover it is said that the itch of passion is greater.
>
> The two parts of the skin of the scrotum divided into two halves are at the sides of the vagina. Likewise, there is a womb in the male's stomach; it is the cause of the swelling of a boy's breasts. In the middle of the phallus manifests a slit; that is the line of the closing of the female organ.

The implication is that because of these similarities it is ridiculous to separate females off as if they were another type of being.

To fortify the eschewing of rigid roles, when he prescribes ornamentation for women he encourages men
to do the same:

> Wear shiny black braids on the sides of the neck.
> Tie a finger-ring on the waist, and wear an anklet
> as an ear ring. The man should equal the behav-
> ior of his woman-friend.

Still, a seeming difference between males and females
is that the former have regenerative fluid but the latter
do not. Gedün Chöpel considers this issue in detail, first
explaining what regenerative fluid is, its function in the
body, and so forth. In Tibetan medical theory there are
seven basic physical constituents—nutritional essence,
blood, flesh, fat, bone, marrow, and regenerative fluid.[1]
Each of the latter is a distillation of the former. As he
says:

> The essence of the human body is blood, and the
> essence of blood is regenerative fluid. Ease of
> body, clearness of mind, and so forth mostly de-
> pend on this essence....Seven drops of the
> essence of food produce one drop of blood in the
> body of a human. From a cupful of blood only
> one tiny drop of regenerative fluid is produced.

Thus, in this system regenerative fluid is not something
that is produced merely in the gonads but arises from
fluids present throughout the body. It is drawn from all
parts of the body through the warm action of two persons rubbing together and emerges from the genitals:

> It is clear that if things having shape are stirred
> and rubbed together, their essence will come out.

---

[1] For a discussion of the seven physical constituents, which
correspond to the seven *dhātu* in Āyurveda, see Dr. Yeshi Donden,
Health Through Balance (Ithaca: Snow Lion Publications, 1986), 52-54.

For example, if two clouds mix, a stream of rain
falls down, and if two sticks are rubbed together,
a tongue of flame appears. Similarly, the essence
of milk is butter, but at first it stays mixed in the
milk. However, if it is poured into a vessel and
churned, warmth arises in the milk in stages, and
its essence comes out separately. Similarly, the
essence of blood is regenerative fluid, but at first
it is dissolved in blood. However, if it is churned
by the action of male and female, the power of
passion raises warmth in the blood, and the regenerative fluid, like butter, comes out.

In contemporary international[1] science also, the ejaculate is composed not just of sperm but of other fluids—
primarily proteins—as is the case also with the female
sexual secretion. Gedün Chöpel emphasizes the importance of this basic fluid, advising his readers to avoid
situations that could compromise its power:

If harm comes to the causes of this essential fluid
from various bad diseases in the body and from
sex with prostitutes and so forth, it is certain the
family lineage of that boy will cease. Parents of
such type will not produce children, and even if
they do, the child will only die quickly; even if the
child does not die, he or she will have physical
problems. Because of this, careful behavior concerning these matters is a necessity.

It is clear that although the Indo-Tibetan medical system
did not know of the existence of sperm, it had a theory
of physical essences that are subject to environmental
and psychological forces. In describing how the regenerative fluid gathers from within the body and is emitted, Gedün Chöpel warns against desisting after intense

---

[1] I am avoiding the term "Western" since this type of study is
prevalent throughout the world.

arousal:

> Wherever the power of the mind gathers, the nerves of that sense organ are drawn together whereby inner fluids are squeezed and are emitted. When a delicious food is contemplated, saliva flows. When embarrassed, sweat flows from the body. When passion is produced, the feminine fluid boils. When happy and sad, tears come from the eyes. Therefore, when beginning to generate passion or sorrow, etc., in the mind, if the feelings are stopped, there is no fault of hindrance, and it is very good. However, when very strong and powerful feelings are produced, if they are stopped with strictness, the force will go to the vital airs at the heart and so forth. If it is looked at from the outside, this is the reason why all those who stay off alone have too much vital air of the heart.

The psychological effect of repressed sexual expression is a gathering of vital airs—i.e., nervous energies—at the heart and consequent neuroses.

Gedün Chöpel reports that there is considerable disagreement in Indian sources on whether women have a regenerative fluid. One view is that women secrete a regenerative fluid slowly during sex, with the result that female sexual pleasure far exceeds that of males. Another view, supported by the author, is that a secretion is being mistaken for a regenerative fluid though he does not question the duration and intensity of female orgasm. He says that it is emitted slowly and not all of a sudden in a single ejaculation as with males, and therefore women are slower to become aroused and do not lose interest so quickly once it is emitted.

All the systems of explanation on whether

women have a regenerative emission disagree.[1]
In the *Sūtra of Teaching to Nanda on Entry to the
Womb*[2] and in the tantras of the New Translation
Schools it is said that women have a regenerative
fluid. The followers of the master Bābhravya[3] explain that from the time of the beginning of the
deed of copulation through to the end women
have a regenerative emission. Therefore, it is said
that if one calculates the pleasure of passion, the
female has a hundred-fold more than the male.
However, others say that the feminine secretion
during passion is being mistaken for a regenerative fluid.

Even if women have a regenerative fluid, aside
from descending by degrees like melting ice, it
does not resemble the way of us men, the sudden
instantaneous emission of a great quantity.
Therefore, women are not satisfied immediately
after its emission and do not experience a reversal of desire as men do. Also, although after it has
been emitted, one continues churning about, a
woman does not find it unbearable, as men do.
One woman says that as the feminine fluid gradually secretes, the vagina becomes moist, and
sensitivity and bliss increase. In that case it may
be that Bābhravya is right [about the greater intensity of women's experience of sexual plea-
sure].

The master Kumāraputra[4] says that male and

---

[1] See the *Kāma Sūtra*, II.1.18-64.

[2] *tshe dang ldan pa dga' bo mngal du 'jug pa bstan pa, āyuṣmannandagarbhāvakrāntinirdeśa*; P760.13, vol. 23.

[3] *Kāma Sūtra*, II.1.32.

[4] *gzhon nu'i bu*. The Sanskrit is conjectured from the Tibetan but I
have not found any reference to such a scholar in Indian erotic literature. Given that the Sanskrit equivalent of *bu* is *putra*, a possibility
is Goṇikāputra, the editor of the fifth part of Bābravya's work.

female do not differ with respect to the emission of regenerative fluid. However, most learned persons nowadays and also women who have studied many books say that the female has no regenerative fluid. Because I like conversation about the lower parts, I asked many women friends, but aside from shaking a fist at me with shame and laughter, I could not find even one who would give an honest answer. Though the goddesses Sarasvatī and Tārā would speak honestly, they definitely do not have any [since they are beyond the world]. When I looked myself, women do not have a regenerative fluid, but there is some secretion. Whether this is a fluid or an air, if an old experienced man investigates, he will know.

Apparently, some Tibetans claimed that the secretion is actually an air, but Gedün Chöpel jokes that if one actually examines it, one will see that it obviously is a fluid.

Because women secrete their sexual fluid differently from men, they have special needs in terms of arousal and stimulation, as will be discussed below. Thus, the recognition of equality does not militate against recognizing differences; the point, rather, is that differences have been magnified out of economic, social, and political motivations into bogus reasons that reinforce sexist discrimination and dominance.

Gedün Chöpel extols the presence of women for the effectiveness and success of activities:

For all activities whatsoever—large and small, for one's own sake, for the general good of the country, for the reign of a king, for the livelihood of beggars—what is indispensable is a woman. Whether making prayer-wishes for the sake of what is wanted or making offering to favored gods, it is said that if one works at these together with women, the effect quickly and inevitably matures.

His view is not a cold appraisal of equality but a warm recognition of the value of females. This is clear from the lyric heights of a description of the female genitalia:

It is raised up like the back of a turtle and has a mouth-door closed in by flesh—the lotus-entrance, burning with the warmth of passion and intoxicating. See this smiling thing with the brilliance of the fluid of passion. It is not a flower with a thousand petals nor a hundred; it is a mound endowed with the sweetness of the fluid of passion. The refined essence of the juices of the meeting of the play of the white and red [fluids of male and female], the taste of self-arisen honey is in it.

4 Sixty-Four Arts of Love

Recognition of both the equality of women and their gradual arousal requires that passionate encounters not be conducted in the all too often male-dominated manner in which the male is concerned merely for his own orgasm. As Gedün Chöpel says:

> Immediately after meeting, entering with ardent desire and immediately after entering, emitting the seminal fluid, this is the way a dog gulps down lungs. Through it not even a little pleasure is found.

He declares that the main point of all of the many arts and techniques of love is to bring the joys of passionate arousal to women and that to do otherwise violates their rights as humans:

> In short, the essence of all these treatises on passion is not to actually perform the act of sex until strong feelings of passion are produced in the woman by various deeds. It is said that signs that the woman has become very aroused are the

rising of the clitoris at the secret gate, shaking,
flesh vibrating, warmth burning, generation of
the feminine secretion, a flush face, and
unmoving eyes. If without the woman's being
wound round completely with passion he forces
himself on her against her wish and does the
deed, it is the way of lower beings, a mass of sin.

Forced sex is a sin against nature because it violates the
needs, wants, and rights of the other party.

Full arousal not only brings pleasure to women but
also enhances that of men, and therefore women also
need to know the sixty-four arts:

If, like fearful thieves eating a meal, a couple just
rubs together quietly and gently on a dark bed
and the regenerative fluid is emitted, it is not a
complete party of passion. Therefore, passionate
men and women should know the sixty-four arts
of passion that bring out the tastes of bliss, various like the tastes of molasses, milk, and honey.
Whatever woman knows well the forms of passion crazing a man's mind and can infatuate him
at the time of pleasure is called the best of
women.

The aim is to stimulate both body and fantasy through
making use of all avenues and recognizing no boundaries:

In short, the places of the body that are usually
not touched by others have great sensitivity. It is
said that the areas from which heat and moisture
arise and all the hollows of flesh that produce
hair are doors of passion.

Again and again gaze at all nine places [ears,
throat, cheeks, armpits, lips, thighs, stomach,
breasts, and vagina]. Bite the nine places. Rub
and suck the nine places. Determine the suitable

and the unsuitable according to your own thought.

Although Gedün Chöpel eschews sado-masochism, he playfully describes the techniques to be used as a battle:

> Making erotic noises, laughing, clamoring, slapping each other, biting and pinching hard, and alternating top to bottom—this is called the battle of male and female in passionate sex. Intoxicated biting, grasping hard, and seeking an opportunity for copulation with rough play—these natural deeds of passion occur in the animals of the forest on up.

Wild activities of passion are to be recognized as part of our nature. They are to be supplemented with deliberate arts so as to increase immersion in pleasure. Gedün Chöpel divides these techniques into two classes—the sixty-four arts and uncertain deeds. He divides the sixty-four arts into eight sections, each having eight techniques:

1 embracing[1]
2 kissing[2]
3 pinching and scratching[3]
4 biting[4]
5 moving to and fro and pressing[5]
6 making erotic noises[6]
7 role reversal, or the activities of the man done by the woman[7]

---

[1] *'khyud pa, upagūhana.*
[2] *'o byed, cumbana.*
[3] *sen mo 'debs pa, nakhacchedya.*
[4] *so 'debs pa, dantacchedya.*
[5] *bskyod cing bsnun pa.*
[6] *sid sgra sgrogs pa, sītkara.*
[7] *skyes pai' bya ba.*

8 ways of copulating.[1]

In the *Kāma Sūtra*[2] Vātsyāyana indicates that he takes the term "sixty-four arts" not literally but metaphorically to indicate loosely that there are a large number of sexual techniques to be described.[3] He reports that in the system of Bābhravya's followers, however, the term is taken literally by dividing the arts of love into eight classes of eight each. Their list of eight includes oral sex as the last and does not give a section for "ways of copulation" separate from "moving to and fro and pressing" as Gedün Chöpel does.

Gedün Chöpel, like Bābhravya's followers, takes the term "sixty-four" literally and employs eight categories of eight each, but he separates out oral sex in an extra class of uncertain deeds that are restricted, or indefinite, in the sense that they are not recommended for all:

> Sucking, slapping, and caressing with the tongue, there are innumerable uncertain deeds, such as *mukhamaithuna* (oral sex), for extremely passionate males and females.

Mukhamaithuna, which literally means mouth (*mukha*) union (*maithuna*), is treated in a separate, final chapter.

Despite agreeing with the Bābhravya tradition in tak-

---

[1] *'khrig stangs/ 'khrig thabs.*

[2] II.2.1-6.

[3] The *Kāma Sūtra* is in seven sections with thirty-six chapters. Following Bābhravya, Vātsyāyana organized the entire book around sixty-four topics—beginning with the contents of the treatise and ending with miscellaneous experiments, charms, and recipes (see Agrawala, pp. 65-69). The sixty-four topics are to be distinguished from the sixty-four arts that Bābhravya's followers used to organize the second section on sexual union. Gedün Chöpel's usage of the term "sixty-four arts" is strictly limited to the varieties of sexual union. The *Kāma Sūtra* (I.3) also speaks of sixty-four arts of a perfect woman beginning with singing and ending with knowledge of gymnastics.

ing the designation of sixty-four arts literally, Gedün Chöpel gives a unique rendition of them replete with evocative detail. Also, he sometimes describes additional postures. Let us identify these individually, giving short descriptions along with their Sanskrit and Tibetan names. (When Gedün Chöpel does not give the Sanskrit, it is provided in the notes if found in the *Kāma Sūtra*.)

FIRST ART: EMBRACING

Gedün Chöpel indicates that the purpose of embrace is to arouse feelings and to remove inhibitions:

Aroused with these forms, women let down
Their hair, kiss, and caress the phallus—
Becoming wish-granting cows fulfilling all
thoughts
Without feigning and embarrassment.

Wish-granting cows are mythical animals that bestow upon persons whatever they wish. The cow, being vital to an agrarian society, is a natural symbol of munificence.

Gedün Chöpel adapts the *Kāma Sūtra*, amplifying and condensing the descriptions and combining Bābhravya's and Suvarṇanābha's lists. Five of his eight forms of embrace—piercing, pressing, twining creeper, tree-climbing, and mixture of water and milk—are somewhat similar to those described in the *Kāma Sūtra* (II.2) as being from Bābhravya.

1 **touching,** *spṛṣṭaka* (*drud pa can*):[1] rubbing against

---

[1] The Tibetan *drud pa can* literally means "rubbing", and from this point of view it aligns with the rubbing embrace (*udghriṣṭaka*) that the *Kāma Sūtra* (II.2.12) cites as being from Bābhravya. Since the Sanskrit *spṛṣṭaka* should be translated into Tibetan as *reg pa can* and not *drud pa can*, the first in Gedün Chöpel's list appears to be a combination of the first, touching (*spṛṣṭaka*), and the third, rubbing (*udghṛṣṭaka*), in Bābhravya's list.

someone seemingly inadvertently.

2 **piercing,** *viddhaka* (*'bigs pa can*): the woman touches her breasts to the man's back.

3 **pressing,** *pīḍitaka* (*gzir ba can*): the man presses the woman against a wall and bites a cheek or shoulder.

4 **twining creeper,** *latāsveṣṭha*[1] (*'khri shing 'khyil ba*): standing stomach to stomach, the man lifts the woman up.

5 **tree-climbing** (*ljon pa'i shing la 'dzegs pa*):[2] standing, the woman puts one foot on the man's foot and another on his waist.

6 **wind shaking the palmyra tree** (*ta la rlung gis bskyod pa*):[3] standing thighs to thighs, the woman shakes her upper body at the male while staring at him.

7 **form of a fluttering flag** (*ba dan g.yo ba'i rnam 'gyur can*):[4] standing or lying down, they embrace, after which she aims her lower body at the man, and they join together.

8 **mixture of water and milk** (*chu dang 'o ma 'dres pa*):[5] naked embrace in bed.

SECOND ART: KISSING
Gedün Chöpel specifies nine areas for kissing:

Ears, throat, cheeks, armpits, lips, thighs, stomach, breasts, and vagina—these focal spots are

---

[1] *Latāsveṣṭitaka* in the *Kāma Sūtra* (II.2.16).

[2] *Vṛkṣādhirūḍhaka* in the *Kāma Sūtra* (II.2.17).

[3] This resembles the thigh-embrace (*urūpagūhana*) in the *Kāma Sūtra* (II.2.24) which is said to be from Suvarṇanābha.

[4] This seems to be Suvarṇanābha's "lower-abdomen embrace" (*jaghanopagūhana*) as given in the *Kāma Sūtra* (II.2.25). Gedün Chöpel does not give the last two in Suvarṇanābha's list, the breast embrace and the forehead embrace.

[5] *Kṣīraniraka* in the *Kāma Sūtra* (II.2.20). According to Upadhyaya (102), the *kṣīraniraka* includes the sesame seed-rice mixture (*tilataṇḍulaka*), which is said in the *Kāma Sūtra* (II.2.19) to be from Bābhravya. Thus, Gedün Chöpel may have subsumed it here.

the nine places of kissing. Determine the suitable and the unsuitable according to your own thought. In particular, the area from beneath the breasts to the knees is tamed by only the touch of sex.

The nine places are somewhat similar to a list given in the *Kāma Sūtra* (II.3.6); Vātsyāyana, however, does not include the vagina in his general list. He mentions kissing the vagina as prevalent in Lāṭa (South Gujarat) and "not fit to be practised by all".[1] Gedün Chöpel similarly calls on his readers to determine for themselves what is suitable and what is not.

The progression of kisses is from the upper body to the lower:

At first kiss the shoulders, then the armpits,
And then slowly move to the stomach.
If greatly aroused and mischievous, kiss the
thighs and vagina.
Draw the water in the canals to the lake.

Kissing arouses and concentrates the force of desire such that subsequent activities become more intense, like the gathering of water in tributaries into a lake.

Gedün Chöpel's section on kissing differs radically from that in the *Kāma Sūtra* (II.3). Although the names of four in his rendition—(1) *pratibodha*, (3) *sphuritaka*, (4) *nimittaka*, and (6) *uttara*—appear in the *Kāma Sūtra*, except for *sphuritaka* the meanings assigned to them are inventive. Gedün Chöpel appears to have taken the *Kāma Sūtra* as a starting point and creatively molded and amplified on it.

1 **mutual acknowledgment,** *pratibodha* (*phan tshun shes pa*):[2] a kiss of mutual acknowledgment as when two

---

[1] Bandhu, 74.

[2] *Pratibodha* is similar in name to *pratibodhika* in the *Kāma Sūtra*

who were previously acquainted meet again.

2 **initial kissing** (*dang po'i 'o*):[1] the man pinches a timid girl's ear and then kisses it and the crown of her head.

3 **throbbing,** *sphuritaka* (*'gul 'phrig can*):[2] a vibrating kiss on the lips.

4 **sign,** *nimittaka* (*mtshan ma can*). The woman rubs the man's body with her lips and tongue, thereby *showing* that she has engendered joy, due to which it is called a sign, a basic meaning of the Sanskrit word *nimittaka*. In the *Kāma Sūtra* (II.3.10) *nimittaka* refers to a young girl's merely touching her lover's lips but out of shyness does not suck his lips, due to which it is translated as "Limited Kiss"[3] and "Nominal Kiss". What in the *Kāma Sūtra* is a kiss in shyness is a kiss of full-fledged desire for Gedün Chöpel.

5 **waterwheel,**[4] *ghaṭika*[5] (*chu yi 'khor lo*): with cheek to nose, a kiss on the mouth, rubbing the inside of the partner's mouth with the tip of the tongue.

6 **after-kiss,** *uttara* (*rjes kyi 'o*): the woman kisses all over the male after (*uttara*) he has done so to her. In the *Kāma Sūtra* (II.3.21) *uttara* refers to "upper"; the woman sucks the lower lip of the man, and the man

---

(II.3.28), but there it refers to a man's kissing a woman, pretending to be asleep, in order to show his desire; hence, Bandhu (77) translates it as "Signaling Kiss".

[1] This faintly resembles *nimittaka* (limited or nominal kiss) in the *Kāma Sūtra* (II.3.10).

[2] This is similar to *Kāma Sūtra* II.3.11.

[3] Bandhu, 74.

[4] The English translation follows the Tibetan. According to Vaman Shivaram Apte's *Practical Sanskrit-English Dictionary* (Poona: Prasad Prakashan, 1957), 419, *ghaṭika* in the masculine refers to a waterman and in the feminine refers to a "a small water jar, bucket, small earthen vessel"; it also means a waterclock.

[5] *Ghaṭika* somewhat resembles *ghaṭṭitaka* in the *Kāma Sūtra* (II.3.12) which, however, means "Touching Kiss" (Bandhu, 74).

kisses the upper lip of the woman; hence, it is trans-lated as "Upper Lip Kiss".[1]

7 **jewel-case,** *piṭaka*[2] (*sprog ma can*): the male sucks and kisses the stomach of the woman lying down.

8 the last kiss, an intoxicated drinking of the emitted regenerative fluid, is unnamed. This does not appear in the *Kāma Sūtra*.

THIRD ART: PINCHING AND SCRATCHING
Pinching and scratching have several functions ranging from sexual arousal to creating a sign that stimulates memory of a pleasurable encounter:

> The purposes of pinching and scratching are to overcome the shrunkenness of the fascinating limb, to distract the mind, to relieve itching in the body, and to convey strong inner passion. It is said that later when parting, if man and woman pinch hard with fingernails on the chest and top of the head, it helps to remember and not forget.

The activity is done in varying degrees—feeling with outstretched fingers, pinching without wounding, deep nail marks, and pinching with wounds:

> To the thighs, behind, and breasts make very red deep nail marks. Feel with the outstretched fin-gers the armpits, top of the head, phallus, and vagina, and pinch without wound. It is also said that at times it is suitable to pinch with wounds the shoulders, neck, and back of the shoulders. It is said that until the wounds heal and disappear, the enjoyment of passion is not forgotten.

Pinching begins in the upper part of the body and moves downward until the time of emission:

---

[1] Bandhu, 75.

[2] The term *piṭaka* faintly resembles *piḍita* in the *Kāma Sūtra* (II.3.25) which Bandhu (76) translates as "Forcible Kiss".

When meeting, pinch the neck and shoulders. When close to entering the vagina, pinch the breasts. When copulating, pinch the back and waist. When emitting, rub the spinal column. As long as he has no embarrassment of the naked woman, as long as he chokes at the throat and the water of desire falls, as long as the regenerative fluid approaches coming out, until then bite and pinch. When the man is approaching emission, the woman's pinching strongly the upper part of his ears will cause the regenerative fluid to come out quickly. Also, sometimes it helps to pinch the armpits.

For some persons pinching so enhances sex that it becomes a necessary part of the act:

Having become accustomed to the activities of pinching, even the deed will not produce satisfaction without it. In many areas passionate women strongly desire the touch of fingernails, and doing the deed without biting and pinching is considered to be like doing it without kissing.

The names of all eight forms of pinching and scratching appear in somewhat different order in the *Kāma Sūtra* (II.4), but the meanings Gedün Chöpel assigns to them are almost entirely different. In the two texts the material after the descriptions of the eight forms of pinching and scratching also differs.

1 **like-scratches**, *ācchurita*[1] (*'phrug dang 'dra ba*): marks like grains of rice on her breasts, made in midst of groans and noises.

---

[1] *Ācchuritaka* in the *Kāma Sūtra* (II.4.12). Bandhu (80) translates it as "Sounding", referring to the sound that the nails make. The basic meaning of the Sanskrit is scratches. Gedün Chöpel's description is more colorful.

2 **long line**, *dīrgarekha*[1] (*ri mo ring po*): first licking with
the tongue and then pressing with the thumbnail
from the vagina to the navel. To appreciate how
vastly different Gedün Chöpel has made his text, one
need only compare his description with that in the
Kāma Sūtra of a mark in the shape of a small line on
any part of the body.

3 **mark of a tiger** (*stag gi rjes*):[2] embracing, they rub
each other's back downwards with the fingernails.

4 **circle**, *maṇḍala*[3] (*dkyil 'khor can*): squeezing his phallus
in the palm of her hand, she presses it with her
thumb while her four fingers circle and press the root
of the phallus. In the *Kāma Sūtra* this is described as
two half moons facing each other; it need not be
mentioned that Gedün Chöpel's description is entirely different.

5 **half moon** (*zla ba phyed pa'i gzugs*):[4] grasping a thigh
and a breast, he pinches with four fingernails.

6 **mark of a peacock's foot** (*rma bya'i rkang rjes*):[5] four
finger marks are made on the nipple and the labia. In
the *Kāma Sūtra* five nails make marks on the breast
and nipple.

7 **marks of a jumping rabbit** (*ri bong mchongs pa'i rjes*):[6]
alternately, they scratch and pinch each other's behind. The *Kāma Sūtra* describes this as marks made
close together on the nipple.

---

[1] *Rekhā* in the *Kāma Sūtra* (II.4.17).

[2] Gedün Chöpel does not give the Sanskrit for "mark of a tiger",
which resembles *vyāghranakha* in the *Kāma Sūtra* (II.4.18), translated
as "Tiger's Claw" (Bandhu, 81).

[3] *Maṇḍalaka* in the *Kāma Sūtra* (II.4.15-16).

[4] Gedün Chöpel does not give the Sanskrit which in the *Kāma Sūtra*
(II.4.14) is *ardhacandraka*. Again, the descriptions do not match.

[5] *Mayūrapadaka* in the *Kāma Sūtra* (II.4.19).

[6] *Śaśaplutaka* in the *Kāma Sūtra* (II.4.20).

8 lotus petals (*utpala 'dab ma*):[1] deep marks are made on the top of the shoulder, between the shoulders, the chest, and the stomach.

Gedün Chöpel reports Indian claims that the sight of marks of scratching and biting causes even the most haughty to melt into lustful reverie:

> Immediately upon seeing the marks of fingernails on the breasts of a young woman and seeing the marks of a woman's teeth on the body of a man, even a queen's thought suddenly wavers, and her composure fades.

Some find it particularly enticing to receive gifts such as flowers and fruits that are covered with scratches and tooth marks:

> It is said that even through giving flowers, fruits, molasses, articles, and so forth despoiled with marks of teeth and fingernails, passion attracts and controls the mind.

FOURTH ART: BITING

Biting comes when passion becomes more intense:

> After they first meet, when passion increases or they approach the time of sex, he should press, push, slap with the palm, pull her hair, and bite.

Gedün Chöpel reports, with reservations, that the leaving of tooth marks on the lower lip of a woman is taken in India to be the equivalent of an adornment:

> The putting of marks like those of biting beneath the lower lips of women is still seen in some parts of India. It is claimed that the amount of passion produced [thereby in the man] is an adornment

---

1 In the *Kāma Sūtra* (II.4.21) this is *utpalapatraka*, which is described as marks on made on the breasts or the waist of the woman.

of the woman.

Through a grammatically unsuitable ending (*yin lo*) Gedün Chöpel indicates his disagreement with this claim.

The first six in Gedün Chöpel's list of bite marks are nominally similar to ones in the *Kāma Sūtra* (II.5.4-18) in slightly different order, but the meanings he assigns to them differ considerably. Gedün Chöpel's sixth seems to combine the sixth and seventh of the *Kāma Sūtra*, but the eighth in the *Kāma Sūtra*, the "boar-bite", does not appear in his rendition.

1 **dots**, *guḍaka* (*thig le can*):[1] having kissed her neck, he squeezes her lower lip between his teeth.

2 **swelling**, *ucchunaka*[2] (*skrangs pa can*): biting the lip such that later it swells.

3 **drops of ambrosia** (*bdud rtsi'i thigs pa*):[3] two subtle tooth marks are set between the lower lip and the chin.

4 **coral jewels** (*byu ru'i nor bu*):[4] marking the cheeks and shoulders with a series of red dots.

5 **series of drops**, *bhindumāla*[5] (*thig pa'i phreng ba*): having pressed the naked woman, the man gazes at her body and bites all the fleshy parts.

---

[1] The term *guḍaka* is somewhat similar in name to *gūḍhaka*, the first of eight bites in the *Kāma Sūtra*, but the latter means "hidden", not "dots". Both texts say that this bite is done to the lower lip.

[2] *Ucchūnaka* in the *Kāma Sūtra*.

[3] In the *Kāma Sūtra* this is *bindu*, described as a teeth-only bite that leaves a spot-like mark.

[4] Gedün Chöpel reverses the order of the fourth and the fifth in the *Kāma Sūtra*. He does not give the Sanskrit for "coral jewels" which in the *Kāma Sūtra* is *pravālamaṇi* and which he may be combining with the sixth *māṇimālā*.

[5] This is a variant for *bindumāla*, which in the *Kāma Sūtra* is a described merely as a series of spots made by the teeth. Gedün Chöpel's expansion is typical of his creativity.

6 pieces of clouds (*sprin gyi dum bu*):[1] teeth-marks one above the other on the upper part of the breasts and the behind.

7 anthers of a flower, *puṣpakeśa*[2] (*me tog ze ba*): the tongue and the lips are sucked hard between the teeth.

8 poplar root (*lcugs ma'i rtsa ba*): with the teeth pressing and rubbing upward on the cheeks, armpits, and areas beneath the navel.

FIFTH ART: MOVING TO AND FRO AND PRESSING

Gedün Chöpel has two chapters on postures of sexual union rather than one as in the *Kāma Sūtra* (II.6). The first is the fifth of the eight branches of sexual arts, and the second is the eight. He substitutes a second chapter on postures of copulation for the chapter on oral sex in the *Kāma Sūtra*, which he treats separately from the eight branches under the heading of uncertain acts.

In this section, Gedün Chöpel describes, not eight, but twenty postures, identifying eight as "fundamental methods of copulation";[3] the other twelve are therefore secondary. There does not appear to be any rationale for separating out certain ones as fundamental; his concern appears to be mere numerical symmetry—eight forms for each of the eight arts.

Four of the twelve secondary postures are given prior to the eight, and the rest, after them. The initial four are found in the *Kāma Sūtra* in the chapter on postures of sexual union (II.6), but not in such detail:

1 crab, *karkaṭaka* (*sbal pa can*):[4] with the woman on her

---

[1] In the *Kāma Sūtra* this is *khaṇḍābhraka*, the seventh bite, described merely as marks on the breasts. Gedün Chöpel's description is more erotic.

[2] The Sanskrit perhaps should be *puṣpakesara*.

[3] *rtsa ba'i 'khrig thabs brgyad po.*

[4] In the *Kāma Sūtra* (II.6.28) this is the seventh of ten postures that Vātsyāyana reports as being from Suvarṇanābha. Two of the vari-

back, the man raises her legs to her lap and does it. Variants are for the woman to hold her legs back, or for the male to tie her feet with a cloth rope and raise them over his shoulders, or for the woman to flap her knees against the sides of the male, or for the woman to assume a cross-legged posture while lying on her back on top of the male.

2 **cow-herd lying supine** (*ba lang rdzi bo'i gan rkyal*): the woman, lying on her back, draws up her knees and spreads her thighs. This is commonly known in the West as the missionary position.[1]

3 **widely opened**, *utphullaka* (*mngon par phyes pa*): kneeling, the woman opens her thighs and with her hands holds the shoulders of the man who, while also kneeling, grasps her breasts; their upper bodies are somewhat distant. In the *Kāma Sūtra* (II.6.8) this is the first of three postures for a woman of the doe type in which the woman puts a pillow under her rear so that her vagina is opened.

4 **Indra's consort**, *indrāṇika* (*dbang mo can*): one thigh of the man is between the two thighs of the woman, such that each squeezes a thigh of the other. In the *Kāma Sūtra* (II.6.8) this is the third of three postures for a woman of the doe type in which the woman brings her thighs up to her sides.

Before giving the eight fundamental postures of copulation Gedün Chöpel offers advice to use a variety of postures:

> With the woman underneath, do it from above.
> With the woman mounting the man, do it.

---

ants offered are similar to the eighth and ninth of Suvarṇanābha's list—pressed (*piḍitaka*) and lotus-like (*padmāsana*).

[1] In the *Kāma Sūtra* (II.6.10) this seems to be the second of three postures for a woman of the deer type called yawning (*vijrimbhitaka*). In the *Kāma Sūtra* (II.6.41) there is a posture called herd of cows (*goyūthika*), but it refers to sex with multiple female partners.

> Similarly, with both lying on their sides, do it.
> Sometimes do it from the back.
> Sitting, do it. Standing, do it.
> Reversing head and feet and embracing, do it.
> Likewise, with a rope of cloth
> Suspend her legs in the air and do it.

He adds a note of caution:

> From among these eight fundamental methods
> of copulation, in the secrecy of your home en-
> large upon whatever you wish. Do not suddenly
> do one which without familiarity and practice
> could hurt nerves, bones, flesh, and so forth.

From among these eight, only two are given in the *Kāma Sūtra*—one in the corresponding chapter (II.6) and the other in the chapter on role reversal (II.8). Gedün Chöpel expands on several of these to the point where it is difficult to determine the boundaries between them.

1 **juice of molasses,** *guḍaudaka* (*bu ram khu ba*): with a cushion under her rear the woman wraps her legs around the man. For variants, see the translation.

2 **powerful,** *sārita*[1] (*stobs dang ldan pa*): the woman, ly-ing on her stomach, puts her legs together, and the man mounts like a horse; she squeezes his phallus hard.

3 **rocking,** *premkha*[2] (*'phul ba can*) and **waving head** (*mgo lcogs can*): the woman, lying on her back, raises the man up with her heels.

4 **pressing down,** *nipātaka* (*shin tu gnon pa*): standing or kneeling, they lean back while touching fingers.

5 **standing copulation** (*langs pa'i 'khrig pa*): while standing, they alternate leaning against a wall and

---

[1] This is found in *The Koka Shāstra*, 137.

[2] This is found in *The Koka Shāstra*, 136. It is given in the *Kāma Sūtra* (II.8.27) as *prenkholitaka*.

doing it from the front and from the rear.[1]

6 **nothing between** (*bar med*): with the woman sitting on a table, she puts her feet on top of his shoulders; he spreads her thighs and does it to the root. A variant is to tie her ankles and put them over his head, or for the man to open her legs with his hands.

7 **partaking pleasure** (*longs spyod can*): with the man sitting in the cross-legged posture, the woman sits on his lap, wrapping her legs around his sides with her feet to the ground; she moves like a swing.[2] For variants, see the translation.

8 **form of a wheel and sound of a bee** (*'khor lo'i gzugs dang bung ba'i sgra*): presumably with the woman sitting on the man's lap as in the previous posture, the man grasps her rear and rotates it round and round.

Gedün Chöpel adds a second set of eight, five of which resemble ones mentioned in the chapter on role reversal (II.8) in the *Kāma Sūtra*:

1 **churning**, *manthana*[3] (*bsrub pa*): the man moves the woman's rear from side and side and in and out like churning butter. In Tibet churns have an up and down motion.

2 **flapping of birds** (*'dab chags bya yi ldem 'gyur*): using his hand, the man moves his phallus in the vagina at various angles.[4]

---

[1] This is similar to the "steady posture" (*sthirarata*) in the *Kāma Sūtra* II.6.35) which is done in a standing position leaning against a wall. Bhattacharya (87) gives this as "Sthitarata".

[2] *'do li'i bskyod pa.*

[3] *Manthana* is mentioned in the *Kāma Sūtra* (II.8.13) in the chapter on role reversal as one of several ways of inserting the phallus in the vagina.

[4] This is similar to "sparrow-sporting" (*caṭkavilasita*) in the *Kāma Sūtra* (II.8.20) described in the chapter on role reversal as one of several ways of inserting the phallus in the vagina.

3 **very powerful,** *hula*[1] (*shin tu stobs ldan hu la*): lying on her stomach, the woman stretches out her legs with her thighs tightly together; the man mounts like a frog.[2]

4 **lustful pangs,** *siṭitaka*[3] (*gdungs pa can*): like a plow, the man moves his rear up and down, parting the vagina.

5 **intoxicating** (*nye bar gzi ba*): the style of a donkey, or ass,[4] in which the two organs meet at the root and the man presses hard for a long time.

6 **motion of a bull,** *vṛṣa* (*glang gi bsgrod pa*): the phallus enters the vagina from the sides and is pressed inside with the tip upwards; the man slaps against the woman's rear.[5]

7 **motion of a horse,** *aśva*[6] (*rta yi bsgrod pa*): the phallus is pulled way out and then inserted to the root with the sound of ripples.

8 **motion of a boar,** *varāha*[7] (*va rā ha yi bsgrod pa*): the

---

[1] Apte (*Practical Sanskrit-English Dictionary*, 1761) describes *hulahulī* as "A kind of inarticulate sound, uttered by women on joyful occasions."

[2] *Hula* is mentioned in the *Kāma Sūtra* (II.8.13) in the chapter on role reversal as one of several ways of inserting the phallus in the vagina.

[3] The Sanskrit given by Gedün Chöpel, *siṭitaka*, is a mystery. *Sītā* (Apte, 1683) means "A furrow, track or line of a ploughshare" and thus would accord with his description of plowing; however, the Tibetan *gdungs pa can* means not "plowed" but "pangs of passion".

[4] Mentioned but not described in the *Kāma Sūtra* (II.6.39).

[5] The *Kāma Sūtra* (II.6.39) mentions but does not describe an elephant posture. In the chapter on role reversal (II.8.19), it describes *vṛṣāghāta* (bull-striking) as one of several ways of inserting the phallus in the vagina, this being how a bull thrusts its horns.

[6] Mentioned but not described in the *Kāma Sūtra* (II.6.39).

[7] This posture is mentioned but not described in the *Kāma Sūtra* (II.6.39). In the chapter on role reversal, the *Kāma Sūtra* (II.8.18) describes *varāhagātha* (boar-striking) as one of several ways of inserting the phallus in the vagina.

phallus is pushed in gently and drawn upward; when completely inserted, the male pushes hard and shakes.

The author advises his readers to rest when tired and encourages resumption of activity until fully satisfied:

> Then when tired, both touch forehead to forehead and rest. Again, with the earlier order perform the play of pleasure until satisfaction.

The aim is clearly not mere orgasm but full immersion in deepening pleasure.

SIXTH ART: EROTIC NOISES

The *Kāma Sūtra* (II.7.8) gives a list of bird and bee sounds that appears to be the source for at least six from Gedün Chöpel's list—pigeon, cuckoo, bee, goose, quail, and dove—but it does not describe these, whereas he does. The *Kāma Sūtra* orients the chapter on erotic sounds around types of striking which give rise to cries, whereas Gedün Chöpel mentions slapping only once. It appears that he sought to avoid violent forms of lovemaking; still, he speaks of hitting or contacting erotic centers through phallic penetration, whereby the woman lets out groans and cries:

> When a focal point of passion is hit, like being hit on the chest with cold water the sound "hoo" of fright will suddenly come forth from a woman. Cold breaths, "Poo, poo," will come out. Sometimes it will be the wordless groan of the stupid and sometimes clear expressive cries. From the burning brighter of the activities of passion there are eight unusual sounds of birds.

The intensity of arousal leads to thrill-cries of profound touch. Pain and pleasure mysteriously meld into each other, yielding an amazing experience of bliss:

By being pressed with strong force, satisfaction is
   produced.
Though pained by the fire of desire, bliss is ignited.
Though crying with unbearable groans, pleasure
   is generated.
O the great nature of amazing bliss!

One of the purposes of identifying various types of cries
is to open the mind to experience the deeper levels of
ecstasy—not to block what naturally arises. Thus, although the eight cries are described as being from
women, they are just as applicable to men.

1 **voice of a pigeon** (*phug ron skad*): the male slaps the
   rear of the female who, embracing and putting her
   mouth to his, emits the sound "noo".
2 **voice of a cuckoo,** *kokila* (*kokki la yi skad*): when the
   head of the phallus touches the bottom of the womb,
   she lets out a cry of passion, "hoo".
3 **voice of a peacock** (*rma bya'i skad*): with unbearable
   passion the woman makes unclear crying noises and
   shouts as if falling down a ravine.
4 **pleasant tone of a bee's sucking honey** (*bung ba
   sbrang rtsi 'jib pa'i dbyangs snyan po*): swooning with
   inexpressible bliss and imagining sky and earth copulating, she lets out a hissing sound, "sa si".
5 **voice of a goose** (*ngang pa'i skad*): when the woman's
   timidity is rent by the sharp needle of unbearable
   passion, she, wanting to be pressed even harder,
   cries, "Pleasure, wealth." In Tibetan the word for
   "needle" (*khab*) also means penis.
6 **voice of a quail,** *lavaka* (*la va ka yi skad*): having been
   penetrated, she becomes overwhelmed and, wanting
   him to pull it out, cries, "Salvation, wealth."
7 **voice of a black goose** (*ngang pa nag po'i skad*):
   ravenous from the tight joining of the two organs
   and wanting to be pressed even more, she cries,

"This is the meaning!"

8 **voice of a dove** (*thi ba'i skad*): the male's entry and withdrawal is so forceful that she shouts so that everyone hears, "The ultimate!"

As will be seen below, from the perspective of Buddhist views of the nature of reality it is not farfetched or exaggerated that in the midst of orgasmic bliss one would cry out, "This is it!" or "The ultimate!"

SEVENTH ART: ACTIVITIES OF THE MAN DONE BY THE WOMAN

Role reversal not only is recommended for passionate women but also is an indispensable form of arousal for some:

> These methods of sex, shifting from top to bottom, are for young women intoxicated with passion. In Malaya[1] and so forth women are accustomed to this and, though honored with gold, will not lie underneath.

Gedün Chöpel also recommends it for weak, tired, or fat males:

> Men who have little strength, are tired, or are fat, as well as women whose passion is very great, do this type of deed with the woman mounting on top of the man. This is known as the woman's doing the work of the man. Old men in India take a young wife and, because they are unable to perform the tasks of the midriff, mostly follow this custom. It is a common custom in many areas.

In order to overcome exaggerated stereotypes of the so-called active and passive natures of males and

---

[1] This is likely the region of Kerala, sometimes called Malaya-deśa where Malayalam is spoken. Thanks to Professor David White for the note.

females—perhaps better described as inserter and receptor—Gedün Chöpel calls on men and women to recognize that each also has traits associated with the opposite sex:

> A male has a little of the nature of a female, and a female has a little of the nature of a male. When mounting on a man, if she has not seen it before, she will look surprised.

Role reversal is not recommended, however, if a couple is seeking impregnation, since the semen has difficulty flowing to the womb when the woman is on top. Also, it is not recommended during pregnancy because of overly agitating the womb:

> It is good to avoid this method if the couple is seeking to have a baby or if the woman is pregnant.

Prior to the eight named postures of role reversal Gedün Chöpel gives four supplementary postures, only the last of which is named. They are:

1 The woman faces the feet of the man with her heels at his armpits and revolves her midriff on his phallus as on a stick.
2 The woman lies back on the man with her head at his feet and revolves her midriff on his phallus.
3 With both squatting, they each put the same thigh between the thighs of the other; the free leg embraces the partner. This can also be done lying or standing.
4 **Scented garden**, *kelaka*: the man sits with feet on floor; the woman sits on his lap with her legs wrapped around his waist; he raises her up and down with his arms. From time to time she rotates her rear, stirring her vagina.[1]

---

[1] About this posture, Gedün Chöpel says:

From among the eight basic postures of role reversal only two of the names are mentioned in the *Kāma Sūtra*—the first in the chapter on postures of sexual union (II.6) and the second in the chapter on role reversal (II.8).

1 **way of a mare** (*rgod ma can gyi tshul*): the woman lies on top of the man whose thighs are opened; she hugs his shoulders and rotates her midriff.[1]

2 **bee, bhramaraka** (*bung ba can*)/**way a bee draws out honey** (*sbrang mas sbrang rtsi 'then pa'i tshul*): the woman either lies on the top of the man as in the previous posture or mounts as on a horse; pressing hard, they embrace and then she rotates left and right and up and down. The Sanskrit term *bhramaraka*

Certain passionate women of the country of Persia are satisfied only through this method of union. It is called scented garden. In the Arbhi language this is known as *kelaka*.

In Tibetan:

> par sig yul gyi bud med chags ldan zhig/
> sbyor thabs 'di nyid kho nas tshim gyur te
> dri zhim skyed tshal bya bar ming btags shing
> ar bhi'i skad du sgrog kel a kar grags

Par sig is Persia or, more specifically, Iran. "Scented garden" (*dri zhim skyed tshal*) suggests the famous *Perfumed Garden* written in Arabic in North Africa by Sheikh Nefzawi for the Grand Vizier of Tunis in the early sixteenth century (and translated by Sir Richard Burton), although I do not know whether the term is used for a specific posture in that text. The word *ar bhi* may be a transliteration for "Arabic". However, *kel a ka* seems to be not Arabic but a transliteration of the Sanskrit word *kelaka*, built from the verbal root *kel* meaning to frolic. *Keli*, for instance, means amorous sport, and *kelīvanī* means pleasure-grove (Apte, 374). *Sgrog* can mean strap or bond or sewing, but what this would have to do with a scented pleasure-grove is unclear (although not impossible to imagine), and thus I have not translated it. I doubt that it means "proclaim" since the sentence also has *grags*.

[1] A mare's posture (*vāḍavala*) is mentioned in the *Kāma Sūtra* (II.6.20), where it refers to the woman's forcibly keeping the phallus in the vagina after it has been penetrated.

means both bee and spinning top;[1] Gedün Chöpel takes it as "bee", whereas the translators of the *Kāma Sūtra* (II.8.25) take it as a "spinning of a top" or "wheeling way", the latter referring to the rotation of a potter's wheel.

3 **dwelling on a boat** (*gru la gnas pa*): with the man lying down, the woman sits on his midriff with her legs to the sides of his chest; joining hands, they move like a swing. The phallus moves in the vagina like the protrusion in the middle of the bottom mill-stone penetrating the top mill-stone and holding it in place.

4 **going and coming**, *gatāgata* ('*gro zhing 'ongs pa*): with the man underneath, the woman mounts with her feet and hands on the ground and her back arched; bending her head down she watches his phallus entering inside the vagina and re-emerging.

5 **sound of a bed** (*khri'u gdangs*): sitting on his midriff, the woman stretches out her legs to the man's armpits. Putting her hands to the floor, she moves like a swing, or they do it like a pestle.

6 **opposite method**, *rodhanika* (*bzlog thabs can*): the man lies down with his upper back on a pillow; the woman wraps her legs around him and hugs his shoulders. They use the pestle and swing movements.

7 **way of taking hold of a pouch** (*rkyal ba 'dzin pa'i tshul*): with the man beneath, he wraps his legs around the woman. The swing movement is used.

8 **opposite method**, *rodhanika* (*bzlog thabs can*):[2] with the man lying down, he pulls his knees up as far as possible; the woman leans back on his thighs and does the work of entering and pulling out. It causes deep

---

[1] Apte, 729.

[2] Why Gedün Chöpel names two postures "opposite method" is unclear, especially since it would seem that all twelve of these postures of role reversal are, in a sense, opposite methods.

penetration and thus is not for pregnant women.

EIGHTH ART: METHODS OF COPULATION
In the *Kāma Sūtra* the eighth branch of sexual union is
oral sex, which Gedün Chöpel treats in a following, separate section entitled "Uncertain Acts". For the eighth
branch he substitutes "Methods of Copulation", of
which all but one (the seventh) are postures of rear-entry. He praises rear-entry for its ability to arouse the
female:

> Because with play from the rear the labia are
> touched and rubbed, arousal is high; therefore, it
> can satisfy with passionately strong pleasure and,
> moreover, can especially bestow bliss on a
> woman.

Gedün Chöpel's emphasis on female arousal is probably
a reason for his substituting rear-entry postures for oral
sex.

Through grouping several sub-postures and variants,
it is possible to determine the eight that Gedün Chöpel
intended. That he names only one—milk cow
(*dhenuka*)—is further evidence of his creative adaptation
of Indian sources. In brief, the eight are:

1 the woman sits on the lap of the man facing away
   from him; he holds a breast and rubs her labia.
2 they do it lying on their sides, from the rear.
3 with the woman lying on her back, her legs are sus-
   pended in the air while the man kneels.
4 the woman sits on the supine man facing his feet.
5 **milk cow**, *dhenuka* (*ba mo can*): with the woman
   kneeling or bending down, the man joins from the
   rear. In the *Kāma Sūtra* (II.6.37) this posture appears
   in the section on the fifth art of sexual union, postures
   of copulation.
6 the woman lies back on the man.
7 the woman sits on the edge of a platform, and the

man does it from the front.
8 the man does it from the rear with the woman lying
on her stomach on a cushion.

Copulation from the rear or with the woman sitting is
recommended for preventing pregnancy:

> In short, all methods of union (1) in which the re-
> productive organ is pointed downward and the
> phallus goes under the vagina and (2) in which
> the waist of the woman is not bent forward are
> helpful for preventing pregnancy. As soon as the
> seminal fluid has come out, the woman should
> rise and pound the floor with her heel. She
> should wash her vagina with warm water; it is
> the same as medicine for the prevention of preg-
> nancy.

Although the Tibetan medical system describes contra-
ceptive medicines, their effectiveness is yet to be
demonstrated in clinical trials.

UNCERTAIN ACTS

Oral sex, which in the *Kāma Sūtra* is the eighth branch of
the sexual arts, is treated in a separate section by Gedün
Chöpel. Perhaps one reason for this is that oral sex, despite its powers of arousal, is limited in its application to
those freed from inhibitions:

> By doing unsuitable deeds, sexual passion in-
> creases like a summer lake. However, with a
> woman who is unacquainted with them and thus
> embarrassed, these unusual methods are com-
> pletely prohibited.

Gedün Chöpel nevertheless recommends that his readers overcome any prejudice against oral sex. To under-
mine the sense that the genitalia and the sexual fluids
are unclean, he appeals to scriptural authority:

An ancient scripture says that whatever comes from the body of a woman during copulation is clean. It is said that a Brahmin, while copulating, should drink the beer of the mouth of a woman until satisfaction.

In an interlinear note he cites the Hindu scripture:

Birds when flying, dogs when hunting, and calves when sucking milk are clean, and likewise [whatever comes from the body of a woman during copulation is clean].

The *Kāma Sūtra*[1] says that the mouth of a dog is clean when it seizes a deer, that the mouth of a bird is clean when it causes fruit to fall from a tree, the mouth of a calf is clean when it sucks milk, and the mouth of a woman is clean for kissing and so forth when engaged in sexual intercourse. These seem to be cases of desires for food and sex pragmatically dominating over cultural perceptions of uncleanliness.

To encourage his readers to experiment, Gedün Chöpel speaks of the prevalence of oral sex in the West and in earlier times in India as evidenced by the number of images of it in temples:

The women of the West are greatly acquainted [with oral sex] nowadays. Previously in the country of India this was prevalent. Most of the old temples of the Brahmins are full of such images.

He also makes reference to those who are practicing a high level of the tantric path (to be discussed below) in which intense sex is used to withdraw all levels of gross consciousness so that more subtle levels—especially the fundamental innate mind of clear light—may manifest. Under such conditions, the seminal fluid is not emitted and remains inside in its channels, heightening the

---

[1] II.9.29.

ecstatic state of orgasm:

> For those intoxicated by inexhaustible pleasure in
> whom the fiery tongue of bliss vibrates inside—
> the essential fluid having been bound in the
> thousand channels—there are no prohibitions.

With lyric beauty he advises that inhibitions be cast
aside:

> Looking at a mirror in front, do it.
> Squeezing a nipple with the teeth, suck.
> With the tongue clean away the dripping femi-
> nine fluid, and so forth.
> Intoxicated and confusing the memory, do ev-
> erything.
>
> Smear honey on each other and taste.
> Or taste the natural fluids.
> Suck the slender and bulbous tube.
> Intoxicated and confusing the memory, do ev-
> erything.
>
> Tell risqué stories.
> Reveal completely the hidden places.
> Think and do embarrassing things.
> Intoxicated and without analysis, do everything.

Similarly:

> Put the flower of feigning behind the ear.
> Give away the plant of doubt as the food of
> birds.
> The female fish of embarrassment is carried
> away by a black female crow.
> Whatever one is not, one is at this time.

And:

> Just as much as a man becomes passionate, so
> much a skillful woman touches, raises, and shows
> her breasts and inebriates him even more with

words of passion. She groans and kisses again
and again and, aiming her chest and lower parts,
embraces. With the form of complete intoxication
and with no clothes at all she makes her body
naked. Then forsaking all attitudes of embarrassment, with the sexy face of burning passion,
she looks at the male's hard phallus. She rocks,
rubs, and strokes it with her hand, inebriating
him.

The theme of overcoming embarrassment runs
throughout the *Treatise on Passion* and is especially rele-
vant to oral sex. Embarrassment traps energy that,
when unleashed, enhances sexual pleasure.

Gedün Chöpel speaks only of heterosexual oral sex,
but the *Kāma Sūtra* sets forth eight types of oral sex for
non-normative males.[1] Thus, it is noteworthy that his
text seems to leave no place for homosexual sex. For
instance, he says:

For every man there is a woman, and for every
woman there is a man.

Also:

This realm of passion is on the level of passion in
which all beings seek passion. The fulfillment of
all enjoyments of passion is just the passionate
bliss of the union of male and female organs.
Who is the man that does not desire a woman?
Who is the woman that does not desire a man?
Except for the difference of external pretension,
all definitely like it.

---

[1] The term *paṇḍaka* (*ma ning*) is usually translated as "eunuch", but
Leonard Zwilling in "Homosexuality as Seen in Indian Buddhist
Texts" (in *Buddhism, Sexuality, and Gender,* edited by José Ignacio
Cabezón [Albany: State University of New York Press, 1992], 203-
214) has shown that the tern has a wider meaning.

And:

> Of those born in this realm of desire
> Both male and female desire the opposite sex.
> The happiness of desire is the best of happi-
>   nesses.
> High and low can find it easily.

More specifically:

> There is no one whose firmness of mind does not
>   diminish
> And whose seminal fluid does not drip
> From looking at and caressing the shoulders,
> Breasts, and genitals of a woman.

Gedün Chöpel's lack of mention of homosexual sex and his deliberate editing out of homosexual oral union that is in the *Kāma Sūtra* is intriguing relative to the preva-lence of same-sex activity in Tibetan monasteries, where he spent half of his life. Perhaps his reticence—he also does not deride homosexuality—is due to his obviously strong attraction to women as well as the often macho attitude in monasteries that same-sex behavior is con-doned as a necessary outlet for pent-up energies in those for whom heterosexual sex is strictly forbidden. The only faint suggestion is found in the above-quoted:

> A male has a little of the nature of a female, and a
> female has a little of the nature of a male.

The concept of self-identity as homosexual is absent in Tibetan culture, as it was in the West until a hundred and fifty years ago. Thus, this book on the arts of love can hardly be faulted for being incomplete in this re-spect. In general, same-sex behavior is not much of an issue in Tibetan culture as long as it is kept discrete.

He gives just one posture of oral sex. The woman lies on the man facing toward his feet with her face in his thighs and his in hers, so that they can perform oral sex

on each other. He says that in Sanskrit it is called
mukhamaithuna (oral union) and that otherwise it is
known as **wheel of whirling pleasure** in that it increases pleasure doubly, quadruply, etc. In the *Kāma
Sūtra* (II.9.34) the position that Gedün Chöpel describes
is called the crow posture (*kākila*), a form of heterosexual
oral sex that is given after the eight postures of oral
union with non-normative males.

Vātsyāyana gives many different opinions on the
suitability or unsuitability of oral sex, whereas Gedün
Chöpel has no hesitation recommending it for those
open to it. He also says that special beings who assist in
the practice of tantra have recommended it for enhancing sexual yoga:

> These deeds [of oral sex] are described in the
> treatises of Female Sky Travelers for the sake of
> satisfying extremely passionate men and women
> who can hold the constitutional essences in their
> bodies without emission.

Female Sky Travelers[1] are special spiritual beings especially dedicated to assisting in the tantric practice of sexual yoga, which involves orgasm without emission. Let
us turn to this topic.

---

[1] *mkha' 'gro ma, ḍākiṇī.*

5 Sexual Pleasure and Spiritual Insight

Gedün Chöpel praises sexual ecstasy as a means for transformation into divinity:

> When the self-arisen blood [the female essence]
>   goes inside the man
> And when the essence of the moon [the male
>   essence] dissolves inside a woman,
> Superior power and bliss are definitely achieved.
> They become like Shaṃkara[1] and Uma.

He describes the act of sex as a sacrament:

> Desiring the fire of passion burning strong, enter to the place of the sacrament of passion. This bed where the friction base of a beautiful woman is laid is just set up for pleasure.

And:

---

[1] Another name for Shiva.

Find release at the great binding thighs.
Press with weight the great door of the lower
   parts where three roads meet.
Put the red top-ornament of coral with burning
   head inside,
And do it to the place of sacrament bestowing
   pleasure on a woman.

He extols the power of ecstatic orgasm:

The glory of the essence achieved from one's
   own indestructible nature,
The taste of honey born from the self-arisen
   body,
This feeling from the play of a hundred thousand
   hairs,
The tongues of gods in heavens have not tasted.

It might seem that he is merely taking poetic license, but
he is not. For instance, he speaks of male and female
deities that are present in the body during sex:

At the time of pleasure the god and goddess giving rise to bliss actually dwell in the bodies of the
male and the female. Therefore, it is said that
what would be obstacles to one's life if done
[under usual circumstances] are conquered, and
power, brilliance, and youth blaze forth. The perception of ugliness and dirtiness is stopped, and
one is freed from conceptions of fear and shame.
The deeds of body, speech, and mind become
pure, and it is said that one arrives in a place of
extreme pleasure.

A frequent theme in the *Treatise on Passion* and in the
Ornament for Nāgārjuna's Thought is the instability and
confinement of conceptions and that release from them
is liberation. As was cited earlier:

Examining through one's own experience how

much attitudes change from childhood through to the decrepitude of old age, how could confidence be put in current conceptions![1] Sometimes even looking at a goddess, one is disgusted; sometimes even looking at an old woman, passion is generated. Something exists now, but later it will not be, and something else will come. Number cannot encompass the deceptions of the mind. When such is understood well, the mind is cut off, and the root of considering the objects of the imagination to be real is destroyed. That is the great relief of bliss; another synonym is freedom.

He emphasizes that reality is beyond conceptual proposition:

As much as one approaches the nature of a thing,
So much do the words of scholars become dumb.
Hence it is said that by nature all subtle phenomena
Pass beyond proposition, thought, and verbalization.

In orgasm the nets of conceptuality melt away into a non-conceptual blissful state of mental clarity:

The necklace of the early clouds of hope and
doubt diminish at midnight.
Melt the moon of the self-arisen basic constituent
into milk.
Give young ladies the great spacious bliss,
Clear and non-conceptual.

The male's regenerative fluid is considered to be in a cold state at the top of the head and thus is compared to

---

[1] This sentence (four lines of verse) is cited in Gedün Chöpel's *Ornament for the Thought of Nāgārjuna* (bod ljongs bod yig dpe rnying dpe skrun khang: 1990), 281.1.

the moon. Through sexual activity it is melted and flows downward, causing the manifestation of subtler and more powerful minds that are used in the spiritual path. Gedün Chöpel makes several references to this process but does not elaborate on it in detail. Therefore, let us draw out the context of Tibetan lore on orgasm, the process of death, and levels of consciousness. My presentation of these will be from standard Ge-luk-ba and Ñying-ma-ba perspectives on Highest Yoga Tantra within the Tantra Vehicle, also called the Vajra Vehicle,[1] one of two basic forms of what is traditionally accepted as Shākyamuni Buddha's teaching.

ORGASM, DEATH, AND SPIRITUAL PRACTICE IN HIGHEST YOGA TANTRA

During orgasm the subtlest and most powerful of all consciousnesses, the mind of clear light, manifests, albeit only unconsciously to the untrained.[2] The *Guhyasamāja Tantra*, a Highest Yoga Tantra that is parallel in importance to the *Kālachakra Tantra*, divides consciousnesses into the gross, the subtle, and the very subtle.[3] We are all familiar with the grosser levels of mind—the eye consciousness that apprehends colors and shapes, the ear consciousness that apprehends sounds, the nose consciousness that apprehends odors, the tongue consciousness that apprehends tastes, and the body consciousness that apprehends tactile objects. To under-

---

[1] *rdo rje theg pa, vajrayāna.*

[2] The section on the mind of clear light is adapted from my "Tantric Buddhism, Degeneration or Enhancement: the View of a Tibetan Tradition", *Buddhist-Christian Studies*, Vol. 10, 1990.

[3] The material on the levels of consciousness is drawn from Lati Rinbochay's and my translation of a text by Yang-ĵen-ga-way-ĺo-drö (*dbyangs can dga' ba'i blo gros*); see our *Death, Intermediate State, and Rebirth in Tibetan Buddhism* (London: Rider, 1979; rpt. Ithaca: Snow Lion, 1980).

stand the perspective of Buddhist thought, it is important to think of these five not just as sensations known
by another, separate consciousness, but as five individual consciousnesses that have specific spheres of activity—colors and shapes, sounds, odors, tastes, and tactile
objects. These five sense consciousnesses are the gross-
est level of mind.

More subtle than the five sense consciousnesses but
still within the gross level of mind is the usual conceptual mental consciousness. In Highest Yoga Tantra,
these conceptions are detailed as of eighty types, divided into three classes. The first group of thirty-three is
composed of emotions, feelings, and drives that involve
a strong movement of energy[1] to their objects. Included
in this group are fear, attachment, hunger, thirst,
shame, compassion, acquisitiveness, and jealousy. The
second group consists of forty conceptions that involve
a medium movement of energy to their objects; among
them are joy, amazement, excitement, desiring to embrace, generosity, desiring to kiss, desiring to suck,
pride, enthusiasm, vehemence, flirtation, wishing to do-
nate, heroism, deceit, tightness, viciousness, non-gen-
tleness, and crookedness. The third group consists of
seven conceptions that involve a weak movement of
energy to their objects—forgetfulness, error as in ap-
prehending water in a mirage, catatonia, depression,
laziness, doubt, and equal desire and hatred. Although
the difference between the first two groups is not obvious (at least to me), it is clear that in the third group the
mind is strongly withdrawn; the three represent, on the
ordinary level of consciousness, increasingly less dualistic perception.

Either through meditative focusing on sensitive parts
of the body or through undergoing uncontrolled processes as in orgasm and dying, the currents of energy

---

[1] Literally, wind or air (*rlung, prāṇa*).

that drive the various levels of gross consciousness are gradually withdrawn, resulting in a series of altered states. First, one has a visual experience of seeing an appearance like a mirage; then, as the withdrawal continues, one successively "sees" an appearance like billowing smoke, followed by an appearance like fireflies within smoke, then an appearance like a sputtering candle[1] when little wax is left, and then an appearance of a steady candle flame. This series of visions sets the stage for the withdrawal of all conceptual consciousnesses,[2] whereupon a more dramatic phase begins the manifestation of profound levels of consciousness that are at the core of all experience.

The first subtle level of consciousness to manifest is the mind of vivid white appearance. All of the eighty conceptions have ceased, and nothing appears except this slightly dualistic vivid white appearance; one's consciousness itself turns into an omnipresent, huge, vivid white vastness. It is described as like a clear sky filled with moonlight, not the moon shining in empty space but space filled with white light. All conceptuality has ceased, and nothing appears except this slightly dualistic vivid white appearance, which is one's consciousness itself.

When, through further withdrawal of the energy that supports this level of consciousness, it no longer can manifest, a more subtle mind of vivid red or orange appearance (called increase) dawns. One's consciousness itself has turned into this even less dualistic vivid red or orange appearance; nothing else appears. It is compared to a clear sky filled with sunlight, again not the sun

---

[1] Literally, a butter-lamp.

[2] The three sets of conceptions correspond to the three subtle minds that appear serially after conceptions cease, but it is not that the three sets of conceptions cease serially; rather, they disappear together, resulting in the gradual dawning of the three subtler levels of mind.

shining in the sky but space filled with red or orange light.

One's consciousness remains in this state for a period, and then when this mind loses its support through further withdrawal of the energy that is its foundation, a still more subtle mind of vivid black appearance dawns; it is called "near-attainment" because one is close to manifesting the mind of clear light. One's consciousness itself has turned into this still less dualistic, vivid black appearance; nothing else appears. The mind of black vastness is compared to a moonless, very dark sky just after dusk when no stars are seen. During the first part of this phase of utter blackness, one remains conscious but then, in a second phase, becomes unconscious in thick darkness.

Then, when the mind of black appearance ceases, the three "pollutants"[1] of the white, red/orange, and black appearances have been entirely cleared away, and the mind of clear light dawns. Called the fundamental innate mind of clear light,[2] it is the most subtle, profound, and powerful level of consciousness. It is compared to the sky's own natural cast—without the "pollutions" of moonlight, sunlight, or darkness—which can be seen at dawn before sunrise. Gedün Chöpel refers to this state as the goal of life:

> Though they have attained the glory and wealth
> of the three billion worlds, they are not satis-
> fied
> And therefore come to be renowned for burning
> ravenous passion.
> In fact they seek the sky-kingdom of bliss and
> emptiness
> With the dumb child of a mind knowing nothing.

---

[1] *bslod byed.*

[2] *gnyug ma lhan cig skyes pa'i 'od gsal gyi sems.*

What people are actually seeking is to consciously experience the state of profound bliss in which all conventional appearances have dissolved in a vast state of ecstasy.

> If one really considers the fact that the one billion
>   worlds of this world system
> Are suddenly swallowed into a gigantic asteroid
>   devoid of perception or feeling,
> One understands that the realm of great bliss
> Is that in which all appearances dissolve.

The ecstatic mind of great bliss is that into which all appearances dissolve and thus is the foundation of all appearance. It is the reality behind appearances that can be accessed in conscious orgasm.

Gedün Chöpel dedicates the virtue, or value, of writing this book to all friendly persons realizing this sky-reality with a mind of profound pleasure:

> Through this virtue may all concordant friends
> Cross the dark path of material desires
> And from the mountain peak of the sixteen pleasures
> See the sky of the meaning of reality.

The sixteen pleasures are degrees of ecstasy that are experienced when, through meditative control, the basic white regenerative fluid that has its source at the top of the head melts and passes down the central channel—first to the throat center and then to the centers at the heart, navel, and base of the spine. The movement to each of these four centers is divided into four blisses each, and thus there are a series of sixteen pleasures, or joys, of increasing intensity. These bliss consciousnesses realize reality which is like a sky into which all appearances have dissolved.

Because the more subtle levels of consciousness are considered to be more powerful and thus more effective in realizing the truth, the systems of Highest Yoga Tantra seek to manifest the mind of clear light by way of various techniques. One of these methods is blissful orgasm because, according to the psychology of Highest Yoga Tantra, orgasm involves the ceasing of the grosser levels of consciousness and manifestation of the more subtle, as do dying, going to sleep, ending a dream, sneezing, and fainting. The intent in using a blissful, orgasmic mind in the spiritual path is to manifest the most subtle level of consciousness, the mind of clear light, and use its greater power and hence effectiveness to realize the truth of the emptiness of inherent existence. As Gedün Chöpel says:

> Having set the mind in the realm of emptiness
>   endowed with all aspects,
> Who could view this wheel of illusory appearances
> With a mind of asserting is and is not
> That even the hand of Buddha does not prevent!

> The small child of intelligence swoons in the deep
>   sphere of passion.
> The busy mind falls into the hole of a worm.
> By drawing the imaginations of attachment
>   downwards
> Beings should observe the suchness of pleasure.

> Wishing to mix in the ocean of the bliss of the
>   peaceful expanse
> This wave of magician's illusions separated off
> By perceiving the non-dual as dual, subject and
>   object,
> Does one not feel the movement and igniting of
>   the coalesced!

Phenomena that are over-concretized such that they seem to have their own independent existence are burnt away in the expanse of the reality behind appearances.

> To what could this reality devoid of projection
>   move?
> Where could this mind devoid of pursuit run?
> Since, having abandoned their nature, they do
>   not stay still,
> Move these two—appearances and mind—in the
>   direction of bliss.

The pleasure of orgasm is so intense that the mind becomes totally withdrawn in and fascinated with it such
that both the usual conceptual mind and the appearances that accompany it melt away, leaving basic reality.
Through consciously experiencing this process, one can
realize that ordinary conceptions and appearances are
over-concretized. Sex, therefore, can become a practice
through which this exaggeration of the status of appearance and mind is identified and subsumed in the
source state.

  In the non-conceptual state of orgasm all of the environment and the beings within it melt in the vast basic
state of the mind of clear light, called the Great Seal:[1]

> May you be protected by the self-arisen Great
>   Seal
> Rolling into one all stable and moving things
> With the lightning lasso of immutable adaman-
>   tine pleasure
> Gone to the one hundred and eight limits.

The fundamental state—which dawns in conscious orgasm—is not a dimming of the mind although it is often
experienced as such because all of the usual conceptual
minds are withdrawn during it. Rather, it is the basis of
all phenomena—the stable (the environment) and the
moving (the beings in the environment); our unfamiliar-
ity with it causes its implications to be missed in uncon-
sciousness. Through developing realization of the

----

[1] *phyag rgya chen po, mahāmudrā.*

emptiness of inherent existence and through developing great compassion, one can become closer to this state. Then, by utilizing this subtle level of mind, the power of the wisdom-consciousness realizing the emptiness of inherent existence is enhanced such that it is more effective in overcoming what prevents liberation from the round of rebirth and all its suffering. Such a wisdom consciousness is also more effective in overcoming what prevents knowledge of others' dispositions and the techniques that can benefit them and thus serves to further the altruistic goals that are behind the quest for wisdom. The theory is that apprehension that phenomena exist inherently or from their own side is the root of all ills because it induces the plethora of counter-productive emotions that produce suffering.

A consciousness of orgasmic bliss is used because, when the experience of pleasure is powerful, one's consciousness is totally involved with that pleasure and thus completely withdrawn; this is the reason why the subtler levels of consciousness manifest during the intense bliss of orgasm, even if many of them are not even noticed in ordinary sex. Without desire, the involvement in the bliss consciousness would be minimal, and thus Highest Yoga Tantra makes use of the sixty-four arts of love-making to enhance the process.

Sexual expression, therefore, can be used as an avenue for exploring the profound nature of consciousness which eventually brings release from craving from the root. Using an ancient example, the process is compared to a worm's being born from moist wood and then eating the wood. In this example (formed at a time when it was assumed that a worm or bug was generated only from wood and heat), the wood is desire; the worm is the blissful consciousness; the consumption of the wood is the blissful consciousness's destruction of desire through realizing emptiness. As the First Paṇ-chen Lama, Lo-sang-chö-ğyi-gyel-tsen, says:[1]

> A wood-engendered insect is born from wood
> but consumes it completely. In the same way, a
> great bliss is generated in dependence on a causal
> motivation that is the desire of gazing, smiling,
> holding hands or embracing, or union of the two
> organs. The wisdom of undifferentiable bliss and
> emptiness, which is this great bliss generated un-
> differentiably with a mind cognizing emptiness at
> the same time, consumes completely the afflictive
> emotions—desire, ignorance, and so forth.

Through desirous activities such as gazing at a loved
one, or smiling, holding hands, embracing, or engaging
in sexual union, a pleasurable consciousness is produced; it realizes the truth of the emptiness of inherent
existence, whereby desire itself is undermined. The
pleasurable consciousness is being generated simultaneously with a wisdom consciousness, and thus the two
are indivisibly fused.

In Ge-luk-ba texts, the undifferentiability of bliss and
realization of emptiness is explained conceptually in
terms of subject and object even though it is beyond all
dualism. The bliss consciousness is the subject that real-
izes emptiness as its object. The reason for making this
distinction is to emphasize that the bliss consciousness is
used to realize the profound nature of reality, the
emptiness of inherent existence—the emptiness of over-
concretization—and thus is not a mere unconscious
mind of orgasm. However, Gedün Chöpel objects to
the treatment of this profound state in terms of subject
and object:

> The easy-to-understand explanation of the union
> of the two—bliss and emptiness—in the manner

---

[1] *Presentation of the General Teaching and the Four Tantra Sets,*
Collected Works, vol. IV, 17b.5-18a.1.

of subject and object varies greatly from the thought of the tantras. Therefore, here regarding the inexpressible meaning that is the final nature of the stable [environment] and moving [living beings], when one considers it from a negative viewpoint it is empty, and when it dawns from a positive viewpoint, it is bliss. Emptiness is a non-affirming negative, and bliss is positive, whereby one may wonder how granting the two of these to one base could be suitable, but one should not fear any reasonings that put their stock in dualistic conceptions.

His point is that when this most subtle level of consciousness is consciously manifested, it knows emptiness of its own accord.

The states of increasing subtlety during orgasm, death, and so forth and of increasing grossness during rebirth, post-orgasm, and so forth indicate levels of mind on which every conscious moment is built. Gedün Chöpel emphasizes that we live in the midst of an unknown glory that can be revealed in sexual ecstasy:

Obeisance to the god of self-arisen pleasure,
Though uncharacterizable, having the aspect of
   characteristics,
Teaching the pure reality to superior beings,
And jesting with the children of darkness.

Obeisance to the god of self-arisen pleasure.
Vivid to those without meditation and to the
   minds of the stupid,
You accompany all and all are your companion,
Seen by all but known by no one.

Obeisance to the god of self-arisen pleasure,
Spatial entertainer not covered with the clothes
   of the conventional,

Having countless magical forms without color
and shape,
Flinging the shooting star of consciousness experienced but not grasped.

Obeisance to the great self-arisen bliss
Where the rainbow lights of the varieties of elab-
orations dissolve,
Devoid of the waves of the ocean of magical illu-
sions,
Where the fluctuating mind does not fluctuate.

Obeisance to the sphere of self-arisen bliss,
Seen by the eyes of Buddhas that never close,
Experienced by the educated upon the severance
of propositional statements,
Comprehended by a non-grasping mind through
the non-elaboration of conceptions.

And:

The thorns of prejudice are only roots of illness.
Without meditation one can cease prejudices,
And an ordinary person will have the bliss of sex.

The aim of the sexual arts is, therefore, not mere repeti-
tion of an attractive state but revelation of the basic reality underlying all appearances.

Nevertheless, the line between the worldly and the
spiritual is difficult to draw:

Taking pleasure in desirable objects is passion,
but taking pleasure in desirable objects is faith itself.[1] Fearing undesirable objects is hatred, but
fearing undesirable objects is renunciation itself.
Whether something is desired or not is a feature
of the mind. Though one tried to change this, it
could not be avoided. Therefore, when examined

---

[1] For a similar point, see La-chung-a-po, 649.12.

carefully, the usage of afflictive emotions in the path is the system of all vehicles.

Passion and faith seem to be completely distinct, but they share the quality of liking their respective objects. Similarly, hatred and renunciation seem to be completely different, but they share the quality of fearing something undesirable. Thus, it is inescapable that religious practices such as faith and renunciation make use of afflictive emotions such as attraction and fear. The worldly realm and the spiritual realm are, therefore, not as distinct as usually imagined.

Indeed, in Highest Yoga Tantra terms for high spiritual states such as "compassion" and "mind of enlightenment" are used with a sexual meaning. Such transference of terminology makes it seem that the inspired altruistic motivation of Great Vehicle Buddhism is replaced with sexual pleasure, but this is not the case in this form of developed tantrism found in Tibet. Instead of substitution, the meaning is that the two exist side by side. Let us take a diversion and consider the usage of the above-mentioned two terms in tantra in order to clarify this point.

In Highest Yoga Tantra the Sanskrit term for compassion, *karuṇā*, is sometimes used to refer to the bliss of orgasm without emission. *Karuṇā* is even viewed as etymologically indicating both compassion and bliss. *Karuṇā*[1] is etymologized as "stopping bliss" (*bde 'gog*) by

---

[1] For a brief discussion of this, see Lo-sang-chö-ğyi-gyel-tsen's *Wish-Granting Jewel, Essence of (Kay-drup's) "Illumination of the Principles: Extensive Explanation of (Kulika Puṇḍarīka's) 'Extensive Commentary On The Condensed Kālachakra Tantra, Derived From The Root Tantra Of The Supramundane Victor, The Glorious Kālachakra, The King Of All Tantras, The Stainless Light'"* (*rgyud thams cad kyi rgyal po bcom ldan 'das dpal dus kyi 'khor lo'i rtsa ba'i rgyud las phyung ba bsdus pa'i rgyud kyi rgyas 'grel dri ma med pa'i 'od kyi rgya cher bshad pa de kho na nyid snang bar byed pa'i snying po bsdus pa yid bzhin gyi nor bu*), Collected Works of Blo-bzaṅ-chos-kyi-rgyal-mtshan, the First Paṇ-chen Bla-ma of Bkra-

adding an anusvāra (ṃ) to the first letter *k*, thereby making *kaṃ*, which means "bliss" (*bde ba*), and by taking *ruṇa*[1] to mean "stopping" (*'gog pa*). Compassion is a case of "stopping bliss" in the sense that finding others' torment in a state of suffering to be unbearable stops, or interferes with, one's own happiness. Similarly, in the Kālachakra system (a type of Highest Yoga Tantra) the great immutable bliss involves a stoppage of the bliss of emission and thus is also a case of *karuṇā*, "stopping bliss", even though, being the great immutable bliss, it is another type of bliss. Both compassion and the supreme immutable bliss are, therefore, cases of "stopping bliss", *karuṇā*. Hence it can be seen that the fact that the term *karuṇā* is sometimes used in Highest Yoga Tantra *additionally* to refer to orgasmic bliss without emission does not rule out its other meaning as the wish that all beings be free from suffering and the causes of suffering.

For instance, the *Kālachakra Tantra* itself speaks eloquently about suffering in the Initiation Chapter (stanza 12) where it says:

> In the womb there is the suffering of dwelling in
>   the womb; at birth and while a child there is
>   also suffering.
> Youth and adulthood are filled with the great suf-
>   ferings of losing one's mate, wealth, and for-
>   tune, as well as the great suffering of the afflic-
>   tive emotions.
> The old have the suffering of death and again the
>   fright of the six transmigrations such as the
>   Crying and so forth.
> All these transmigrating beings, deluded by illu-
>   sion, grasp suffering from suffering.

śis-lhun-po, (New Delhi: Gurudeva, 1973), vol. 3, 35.5-36.1.

[1] Not found in the Apte dictionary.

Moreover, the tantric vows, taken during the initiation ceremony, call for practitioners to commit themselves to liberating all beings:

I will liberate those not liberated [from the obstructions to omniscience].
I will release those not released [from cyclic existence].
I will relieve those unrelieved [in bad transmigrations]
And set sentient beings in nirvana.

Also, that altruism is at the very heart of the initiation ritual is clear from the fact that the process begins with an adjustment of motivation toward altruism and ends with authorization to teach by way of the wise altruism that takes account of individual predispositions and interests.[1] Thus, the special meaning of *karuṇā* in Highest Yoga Tantra as the bliss of orgasm without emission does not supplant the meaning of *karuṇā* as compassion.

The Mongolian scholar and yogi, Jang-ḡya-rol-bay-dor-jay,[2] lama to the Ch'ien-lung Emperor during the Manchu domination of China in the eighteenth century, emphasizes that the practitioners for whom tantra was specifically taught are even more compassionate and of a higher type than the practitioners of the sūtra version of the Great Vehicle. In his *Clear Exposition of the Presentations of Tenets*, he says:[3]

It is said in the precious tantras and in many commentaries that even those trainees of the

[1] In Tenzin Gyatso and Jeffrey Hopkins, *The Kālachakra Tantra: Rite of Initiation for the Stage of Generation* (London: Wisdom Publications, 1985; second revd. edition , Boston 1989), see the beginning of the ritual, pp. 170-174. Also, for the end of the ritual, see my introduction, p. 124, middle, as well as the ritual, pp. 333-338.

[2] *lcang skya rol pa'i rdo rje*, 1717-86.

[3] As cited in *The Kālachakra Tantra, Rite of Initiation*, p. 33.

Mantra Vehicle who have low faculties must
have far greater compassion, sharper faculties,
and a more superior lot than the trainees of
sharpest faculties in the Perfection Vehicle.
Therefore, those who think and propound that
the Mantra Vehicle was taught for persons dis-
couraged about achieving enlightenment over a
long time and with great difficulty make clear
that they have no penetration of the meaning of
tantra. Furthermore, the statement that the
Mantra Vehicle is quicker than the Perfection
Vehicle is in relation to trainees who are suitable
vessels, not in terms of just anyone. Therefore, it
is not sufficient that the doctrine be the Mantra
Vehicle; the person must be properly engaged in
the Mantra Vehicle.

Jang-ġya emphasizes that the mere wish of a practitioner to practice tantra is not sufficient; the person
must be *capable* of its practice. Far from being taught for
those who are unable to proceed on the Perfection
Vehicle, the tantras were expounded for persons of
particularly great compassion.

In a similar vein, the Seventh Dalai Lama says that
practitioners of Mantra are especially motivated by
compassion, intent on the quickest means of attaining
the highest enlightenment in order to be of service to
others:[1]

Some see that if they rely on the Perfection
Vehicle and so forth, they must amass the collec-
tions [of merit and wisdom] for three countless
great eons, and thus it would take a long time
and involve great difficulty. They cannot bear
such hardship and seek to attain Buddhahood in
a short time and by a path with little difficulty.

---

[1] As cited in *The Kālachakra Tantra, Rite of Initiation*, pp. 31-32.

These people who claim that they, therefore, are engaging in the short path of the Secret Mantra Vehicle are [actually] outside the realm of Mantra trainees. For to be a person of the Great Vehicle in general, one cannot seek peace for oneself alone but, from the viewpoint of holding others more dear than oneself, must be able, for the sake of the welfare of others, to bear whatever type of hardship or suffering might arise. Since Secret Māntrikas are those of extremely sharp faculties within followers of the Great Vehicle, persons who have turned their backs on others' welfare and want little difficulty for themselves are not even close to the quarter of Highest Secret Mantra....One should engage in Highest Yoga Tantra, the secret short path, with the motivation of an altruistic intention to become enlightened, unable to bear that sentient beings will be troubled for a long time by cyclic existence in general and by strong sufferings in particular, thinking, "How nice it would be if I could achieve right now a means to free them!"

Even though the path of the Mantra Vehicle is quicker and easier, a practitioner cannot seek it out of fearing the difficulties of the longer sūtra path. Rather, the quicker path is sought due to being particularly moved by compassion; a Mantra practitioner wants to achieve enlightenment sooner in order more quickly to be of service to others.

Just as the unusual usage of *karuṇā* to mean the bliss of orgasm without emission does not cancel its also meaning compassion in other contexts, so the term "mind of enlightenment" (*bodhicitta*) also has an unusual meaning that does not rule out its having, in other passages of Highest Yoga Tantra, its usual connotations. The term "mind of enlightenment" has as its broadest referents the conventional mind of enlightenment, which is the altruistic intention to become enlightened, and the ultimate mind of enlightenment, which is a wisdom consciousness in the continuum of a Bodhisattva directly realizing emptiness. However, the term "mind of enlightenment" is also used to refer to semen or, more accurately, to the white and red essential or regenerative fluids of both males and females. This unusual usage of "mind of enlightenment" for basic regenerative fluids does not cancel out its more usual meanings, for altruism and realization of emptiness are the very basis of the fundamental tantric meditation of deity yoga.[1] Rather, as with *karuṇā*, the term *bodhicitta* is used additionally *in specific circumstances*, to refer to the essential white and red fluids of male and female.

Since the tradition holds that only the most compassionate are capable of practicing Highest Yoga Tantra, which involves using the bliss arising from union of male and female in the path, it clearly posits a connection between the capacity of compassion and the capacity to use sexual bliss in the path, but it does not reduce the high motivations and realizations of Great Vehicle Buddhism to ordinary states. Gedün Chöpel similarly does not abandon the profundity of the sacred when he points out the frequent overlap between the secular and the religious realms. He is, however, critiquing those who separate such feelings as desire and faith as if attraction did not influence faith. He is also emphasizing the basic tantric doctrine that a mind of orgasm can yield a vision of reality and thus that the realms of the mundane and supramundane are not entirely different.

In a more general way, Gedün Chöpel explains that sex is meaningful on two levels, a worldly one in the engendering of family lineages and a spiritual one in the practice of experiencing bliss and the emptiness of

---

[1] For discussion of this topic, see Jeffrey Hopkins, *The Tantric Distinction* (London: Wisdom Publications, 1984).

inherent existence:

> Alas, I am crazy nowadays, and though those who are not will laugh at me, the experience of bliss is not of little meaning, and the birth of family lineages is not of little meaning. If one can sustain the way of passion from within bliss and emptiness, how can that have little meaning?

In the same vein:

> Because it gives an excellent lineage and the glories of pleasure and because it is the essence of life and has the nature of one's innate deity, it is said that even slight prohibition of intoxicating deeds at the time of pleasure is a sinful doctrine.

In a worldly way, family lines are important as is the relief that pleasure brings. The spiritual meaning is that within sustaining the pleasure of passion, bliss and emptiness can be experienced. The question is *how* to sustain sexual pleasure so that its spiritual value is not lost and the experience turns into an unconscious dimming of mind. Gedün Chöpel hints at this when he calls for the removal of all inhibitions.

By forgoing cultural prohibitions, sexual pleasure can be extended such that it penetrates the entire physical structure:

> Having clearly seen the intoxicating lotus of ambrosia between her plump thighs, like a spring bull penetrate a girl, a pool of desire. Press with the chest a passionate girl with curvaceous waist and movement swift like a fish. By swimming in the lake of passion even the particles of the body become just blissful and joyous.

To experience the union of bliss and emptiness, sexual pleasure has to be developed in fullness, and to do this it is also necessary to implement techniques for avoiding premature ejaculation and extending the experience of pleasure. Otherwise, a valuable opportunity is lost in the ephemerality of orgasm. One technique is to pause in the midst of intense feeling and let the feeling of bliss pervade the body:

> If one does not know the techniques of holding and spreading the bliss that has arrived at the tip of the jewel [i.e., the head of the phallus], immediately upon seeing it for a moment it fades and disappears, like picking up a snowflake in the hand. Therefore when, upon churning about, bliss is generated, cease movement, and again and again spread [the sense of bliss throughout the body]. Then, by again doing it with the former methods, bliss will be sustained for a long time.

He explains that speedy ejaculation is due to concentrating too strongly on the region of the genitals:

> If when bliss spreads throughout the body, one can stop the attention from going to the lower parts and can experience with the mind the feeling of bliss only of the upper body, the regenerative fluid will not diminish no matter how much one plays. The causes and conditions of losing the regenerative fluid derive from not experiencing in a broad and vast way the bliss fully pervading the body and, instead of that, aiming the mind to the bliss of only the private parts.

Techniques to enhance the power of pleasure include wiping each other's genitalia with a cloth, using various postures of copulation, and directing one's attention to the upper part of the partner's body when the intensity of pleasure increases in the lower parts:

> From time to time, both should wipe the private parts well with a clean cloth. Then do it, shifting

among various methods of copulation, and the bliss will become very powerful. Hold the regenerative fluid a long time by looking with eye and mind at a spot in the middle of the woman's brow and at her face and by strongly asking and answering words of passion.

One can imagine the sky, thereby moving the mind away from the genitalia:

> When the fluid arrives at the root of the male sign, the lower parts become heavy and numb; hence, at that time imagine the expanse of the sky and pull inward strongly, whereby its reversal will be certain.

Gedün Chöpel also advises the male to contract his limbs and pull in his stomach when ejaculation is imminent:

> Close the lower gate [the anus], and turn the tongue and eyes upwards. Contract the joints of the feet and hands, and tighten the fingers strongly. Pull in the stomach to the backbone. These are physical techniques that should be done.

Distracting the mind to neutral topics such as the multiplication table can help:

> Aim the mind at the multiplication table—eight times three is twenty-four, six times five is thirty, and so forth. Also, if the woman pinches him and emphatically says, "Look here," he will be able to bind the regenerative fluid.

Through such techniques of strengthening and lengthening sexual pleasure, both mind and body become bathed in bliss, opening the possibility of realizing the nature of the fundamental state. These are common methods for delaying ejaculation and should not be confused with meditative techniques used in tantric practice for preventing ejaculation by causing the regenerative fluid to be withdrawn back into the structure of channels after it has arrived at the tip of the phallus. Gedün Chöpel deliberately does not mention such specifically tantric techniques due to their secrecy:

> Here [in this book] there has been no proclamation of the secret—the profound modes of practice, the vocabulary, and so forth of Secret Mantra. Nevertheless, with diligence embarrassing deeds should just be kept secret from others.

Though the tantric doctrine of the fundamental innate mind of clear light is basic to his presentation of the arts of love, he does not transgress the bounds of secrecy concerning tantric techniques that can only be performed by those capable of controlling bodily processes through meditative control of the energies that drive them.

The Ñying-ma-ba doctrine that the blissful mind of clear light pervades all experience and is accessible within any state is the theoretical underpinning of Gedün Chöpel's advice to extend the intense state of sexual bliss in order to explore the fundamental state of bliss. Even if emission is not stopped, such exploration is possible before, during, and after emission.

Indeed, that all human endeavors are for the sake of pleasure is not happenstance; they have, behind them, the quest for profound bliss:

> Even taking a single step is for the sake of seeking bliss.
> Even speaking a single word is for the sake of seeking bliss.
> Virtuous deeds are done for the sake of bliss.
> Non-virtuous deeds also are done for the sake of bliss.

Eyeless ants run after bliss.
Legless worms run after bliss.
In short, all worldly beings one by one
Are running, faster and slower, in the direction of
bliss.

Still, the state of innate bliss is hard to bear:

Though there are many sufferings hard to endure,
There is no bliss harder to bear other than this.

Conceptual over-concretization of objects prevents realization of the most profound and ecstatic state by generating attachment to superficial, unreal exaggerations.
This attachment, in turn, fosters an inability to sustain
the basic, blissful state that undermines emotionally
imbedded self-deceptions. The suggestion is that ordinary conscious life is concerned with only the gross or
superficial, without heed of more subtle states that are
the foundation of both consciousness and appearance.
We know neither the origin of consciousness nor the
basis into which it returns.

Ordinary beings are so identified with superficial
states that the transition to the deeper involves even
fear of annihilation; when the deeper states begin to
manifest and the superficial levels collapse as in the process of dying, we panic, fearing that we will be wiped
out and, due to this fear, swoon unconsciously. As the
late eighteenth- and early nineteenth-century
Mongolian scholar Ngak-w̄ang-kay-drup[1] says in his
Presentation of Death, Intermediate State, and Rebirth,[2] at
the time of the clear light of death ordinary beings generate the fright that they will be annihilated. The fear-in-

---

[1] *ngag dbang mkhas grub*; 1779-1838. Also known as *kyai rdo mkhan po*.

[2] *skye shi bar do'i rnam bzhag*, Collected Works (Leh: S. Tashigangpa,
1973), Vol. 1, 466.2. Cited in Lati Rinbochay and Jeffrey Hopkins,
Death, Intermediate State, and Rebirth in Tibetan Buddhism, 47.

spiring aspect of its manifestation accords with the often described awesomeness and sense of otherness that much of world culture associates with types of profound religious experience. The fact that the mind of clear light—which is so awesome when it newly manifests—is one's own final nature suggests that the otherness and fear associated with its manifestation are not part of *its* nature but are due to the shallowness of untrained beings. The strangeness of our own nature is a function of misconception, specifically our mistaken sense that what are actually distortions of mind subsist in the nature of mind. We identify with these distortions such that when basic consciousness starts to manifest either in orgasm or in dying, we are unable to remain with the experience. The more we identify with distorted attitudes, the greater the fear of the foundational state.

Gedün Chöpel advocates the usage of sexual pleasure to open oneself to this profound, fundamental state at the core of all consciousness:

> Alas, the king of pleasure gives the path of life
> To the women of the world.
> Take the power of a life wishing for the hard and
>   stable
> To this whirlpool of passion with waves of love.

The "hard and the stable" are the over-concretized phenomena in which we falsely put our aspirations. Rather than pinning our hopes on such exaggerations, the force behind the wish for solidity should be allowed to dissolve in the swirl of love. This profound level of bliss, although at first hard to bear, has within it a source of sustenance beyond the dualism of subject and object.

6 *Ethic of Love*

An ethic of love is intrinsically communicated in the
Treatise on Passion. It is based on non-denial of basic facts
including the context of suffering. It is founded on non-
coercion, non-pretentiousness, and non-deceit. It calls
for mutual respect between partners and constituted by
a caring relationship that promotes comfort and happiness. Let us discuss these.

NON-DENIAL OF BASIC FACTS

In stressing that all of us come from a procreative act,
Gedün Chöpel calls his readers to appreciate a basic fact
often ignored by religious systems that suppress sexual
expression:

> If they were not joined by the relationship of
> copulation, the male and the female sexes would
> be separate. Thus in the world there would be
> two parties, and they would be certain to live in
> war and controversy. Monks who live in the soli-
> tude of hermitages indeed do not understand the

121

value of this, but even the dependent-arising in which a life-support with the eighteen types of leisure and fortune is attained comes first from this. It is said that if sex were abandoned, this world would definitely become empty in a moment. If there were no human beings, how could there be monks and the Buddhist teaching?

In Buddhism a life that has all factors allowing for successful spiritual practice is said to be endowed with leisure and fortune. Leisure[1] means to be free from the eight conditions of non-leisure:[2]

1 birth as a hell-being
2 birth as a hungry ghost
3 birth as an animal
4 birth in an uncultured area
5 possessing defective sense faculties
6 having wrong views
7 birth as a god of long life
8 birth in a world system where a Buddha did not come.

Fortune[3] is tenfold; the five inner fortunes are:

1 being a human
2 being born in a place where Buddhist teaching flourishes
3 having sound sense faculties
4 not having done the five actions of immediate retribution in a hell after death: killing one's father, killing one's mother, killing a Foe Destroyer,[4] with bad

---

[1] *dal ba, kṣaṇa.*

[2] *mi khom pa, akṣaṇa.* The chart is taken from Geshe Lhundup Sopa and Jeffrey Hopkins, *Cutting Through Appearances: The Practice and Theory of Tibetan Buddhism* (Ithaca: Snow Lion Publications, 1990), 24.

[3] *'byor pa, saṃpad.*

[4] *dgra gcom pa, arhat/ arhan.*

intention causing blood to flow from the body of a Buddha, and causing dissension in the Spiritual Community
5 having faith in Buddha's scriptures.

The five outer fortunes are:

1 a visitation from a Buddha
2 his teaching the excellent doctrine
3 his teaching remaining to the present
4 his followers still existing
5 the people of the area having mercy and love for others and thus teaching others.

Gedün Chöpel mockingly opines that if Buddhists value such a life so highly they should also value the act of copulation that gives rise to all of these.

The mockery continues:

> The two superior persons and the six scholars who were like ornaments were born in the country of India. The teacher [of Bön], Shen-rap,[1] was born in the area of Öl-mo.[2] A Ming Emperor was born in a palace in China. One does not need to explain where they actually came from.

The "two superior persons", Guṇaprabha and Shākyaprabha, are famed Indian scholars of the division of Buddha's scriptures called discipline.[3] The "six ornaments" are Indian scholars who framed much of the tradition—Nāgārjuna, Āryadeva, Asaṅga, Vasubandhu, Dignāga, and Dharmakīrti. All of these are said to have come from certain places, but all in fact came from the wombs of women.

In a similar vein:

---

[1] *gshen rab.*
[2] *'ol mo.*
[3] *'dul ba, vinaya.*

Non-Buddhist books say that the Brahmin caste
was produced from the mouth of Brahmā. This is
difficult to accept as true, but no one, clever or
stupid, can deny that all four castes are born
from the genitals of women.

He complains that prohibition runs contrary to the basic
nature of humans:

For every man there is a woman, and for every
woman there is a man. In the mind of both there
is desire for sex. What chance do those living
with clean rules have? By prohibiting suitable
deeds in actuality and by promoting unsuitable
deeds in secrecy, how can religious and worldly
morality suppress this natural passion of humans!
How could it be correct to prohibit as faulty the
bliss naturally abiding in the nerve-structure of
the five chakras in the vajra-city of six essences!

The "five chakras" are nerve centers at the top of the
head, throat, heart, navel, and base of the spine. The
"vajra-city" is the body, and the "six essences" are—according to one interpretation—earth, water, fire, wind,
channels, and drops. According to another interpretation, they are bone, marrow, and regenerative fluid obtained from the father, and flesh, skin, and blood obtained from the mother.[1] In ordinary sex, essential fluids
in this nerve-structure gather and pass through certain
areas that generate pleasure, and in tantric yoga,
through concentrative focusing on these centers the
subtler levels of mind become manifest. Gedün Chöpel
suggests that since it is within this natural framework
that sacred realizations can be gained, one should respect such a natural endowment.

Gedün Chöpel is at once explaining (or rationalizing)

---

[1] See Lati Rinbochay and Jeffrey Hopkins, *Death, Intermediate State,
and Rebirth in Tibetan Buddhism*, 30.

his own situation as a monk who gave up vows of celibacy and prescribing a perspective on desires that naturally abide within. His description of the pangs of desire is vividly poignant:

> The suffering of not getting one's desire is a burning of the bones night and day; though for a young man this suffering is great, his elders always treat it as unimportant. Even more, girls who are protected and bound by their parents have this suffering beyond measure. Therefore, when they arrive at a suitable age, male and female definitely need a way to live together.
>
> The passion of a young woman for a man does not even compare with the thirsty's yearning for water. A passionate man's contemplation of a woman does not even compare with the hungry's desire for food. Prevention by strict parents does not even compare with being put into a dark hole. Being constrained by strict rules does not even compare with being put in stocks.

The imagery of restraint is so severe that it might seem that Gedün Chöpel opposed the taking of vows of celibacy, but his point is that individual differences need to be respected, without coercion:

> It would be better for the carnivorous wolf and the grass-eating rabbit, rather than comparing each other's advice on the topic of food, to further their own individual style of behavior among agreeable companions of similar type. There is no sense in urgently exhorting people to do what they do not wish—[asking] nomads to eat pork, city-folk to drink melted butter, and so on. There is also no sense in strictly preventing what one desires. The good and bad, the clean and the dirty are only one's own fancy. One should proceed, always shifting among desired

activities. Debating and arguing about these will only wear one out. Analyzing for reasons will eventually afflict [one's own mind].

Even though he decries suppression, he praises those who, upon perceiving the suffering that is endemic to lifetimes bound in a process of repeated birth, aging, sickness, and death, take vows and train in the basic spiritual triad of ethics, meditative stabilization, and wisdom:

> If, having seen the depths of the ocean of cyclic existence, one cannot bear the sadness due to wishing to leave it, one should take the life of a saffron-robed [monk or nun] and become solely absorbed in the doctrine of peace. Tibetan scholars in the good eras of yore came to India, the country of Superiors; they possessed the three learnings and bound the three doors [of body, speech, and mind with vows]. However, [nowadays] it is hard to bear even hearing talk about such.

Consonant with the Buddhist theory that the times are worsening, he complains that nowadays people cannot even bear to hear about the constraint that such training involves.

Nevertheless, he indicates the pointlessness of restraint if it is not done consciously out of recognizing the suffering of cyclic existence, and he derides those who maintain only the outer pretension of keeping vows:

> The good foolish man who himself binds himself with chains, not through renunciation, not through religion, not through the right way, and not through vows, uses up his life this way. Similarly, the hidden deeds of those passionate persons in disguise—making effort at pretension

and so forth—are said to be just axes chopping away at their basic physical constituents.

Deceit about sexuality turns against the perpetrator, undermining physical health.

Similarly, failing to recognize dammed up passions is fruitless and counter-productive since passions eventually will break free:

> If one's expertise in renunciation is not complete, [one's passion is like] a great river which, though stopped by a dam, just breaks loose. Still, if renunciation is like a levying of taxes under an unwanted regulation, it is like trying to pull great stones uphill.

Turning away from suppression of sexual attraction and to expression of desire, however, is not to be done within denial of the basic context of suffering:

> When experience has been gained over a long time, there is nothing that does not sadden the mind in terms of this lifetime. Relieving a saddened mind is the divine religion of the excellent. Eventually, it comes down to what is done with the mind.

When one examines closely one's own life, it is seen to be a mass of discouraging suffering. As the Fourth Panchen Lama says:[1]

> Once one has taken birth in cyclic existence due to [former polluted] actions and the afflictive emotions [of desire, hatred, and ignorance], one does not pass beyond suffering. Because enemies become friends and friends become enemies, there is no certainty about someone's helping or

---

[1] Geshe Lhundup Sopa and Jeffrey Hopkins, *Cutting Through Appearances: The Practice and Theory of Tibetan Buddhism* (Ithaca: Snow Lion, 1990), p. 76.

harming. However much the happiness of cyclic existence is enjoyed, not only is there no final satisfaction, but also attachments are extended, bringing about many unbearable sufferings. However good a body one obtains, as it must be given up again and again, there is no certainty with regard to obtaining a certain type of body. Because the gap between lives is closed again and again beginninglessly, the limits of birth are not to be seen. No matter what prosperity of cyclic existence is obtained, because finally it must definitely be forsaken, there is no certainty with regard to obtaining prosperity. Because one must go alone to the next life, there is no certainty with regard to friends.

According to standard Buddhist doctrine, it is religion that brings solace in the midst of such pain. Gedün Chöpel's provocative point is that a loving relationship is like religion in that it brings some relief from pain.

Still, he is not turning Buddhism on its head. For him, love is to be sought within understanding that one is bound in a process of suffering that becomes even worse if consumed by craving:

The lake Manasarowara which is said to be huge by those who have not seen it is a bird's puddle when one arrives nearby. When one bends and tastes the phenomena of cyclic existence, it is so true that there is no amazing essence. However, there are neither fewer nor more men than women, and each is easy to find. If one wishes the other, the sin of craving is greater than that of doing it. Hence, it is right to partake of the enjoyments of sex in all ways.

The basic Buddhist notion of attempting to abandon craving is maintained but within wise recognition that if prohibition of sex is mere external pretension, the inner craving creates negative karma. This realism—facing facts—is the basis of the ethic of love in the *Treatise on Passion*.

NON-COERCION AND NON-PRETENSION

Non-coerciveness is also fundamental, as is evidenced by Gedün Chöpel's repeated emphasis on enhancing the pleasure of women and not just using them as avenues for male orgasm. He stresses that even if passion is not a virtue from the viewpoint of the Buddhist presentation of the process of suffering, it is devoid of harmfulness and thus certainly not a non-virtue:

> Among men and women who have lost all wealth and power, even an old man whose head is whiter than a conch experiences unspeakable pleasure in the vagina of an old woman. In passion there is no constraining or beating with bad thought and there is no stabbing with the spear of a harmful mind. Though there is no virtue in giving passion to a being of the realm of desire, from where could any sin come?

He advocates non-self-centeredness, in which only appropriate techniques are used:

> The following are techniques of pleasure posited for powerful men and passionate women so that they may sustain mental deeds, according to wish, upon entering the wheel of intrepid desire. One should use a method of sex suitable for the occasion, having understood well the customs of various areas and the different constitutions of individual women.
>
> Those who have just given birth, those suffering in pregnancy, those who are ill, those with great worry, and those who are very old or very

young are never suitable for the deeds of passion.

At the heart of this ethic of love is mutuality, a non-hierarchical perspective that is built on realizing vital common qualities shared by all:

> The stupid who cherish unfabricated appearances and the clever who create fabricated imaginations split off from discordant paths, but again at the end of the three paths [past, present, and future] come together.

Recognition of common qualities depends upon eschewing pretension:

> Beggars frown on gold, and hungry guests spit at food. Sex is disclaimed from the mouths of all, but it alone is what is liked from the minds of all.

And:

> The innate bliss is non-artificial and self-arisen, but all the world wears a mask of pretension. Therefore, at the time of pleasure male and female should abandon all customs and feigning.

Prejudices of what is clean and what is dirty must be overcome:

> Who can distinguish the clean and the dirty in the upper and lower parts of the body? By what can the upper and lower parts of the body be assigned as good or bad? That the upper part is satisfactory and the lower part is hidden is unremarkable good behavior.

He advises opening the mind to full sexual expression through sharing sex games with partners:

> This passion which comes to all men and women without striving and by their very nature is

covered with a little embarrassment; if one makes a little effort at it, its nature will nakedly show itself. Look at a drawing of a sleeping nude; look at horses and cattle copulating; write out and read treatises on passion; tell various stories of passion.

Culture-bound attitudes of embarrassment prevent manifestation of a loving relationship, in the fullness of which sexual pleasure is enhanced.

CREATING MUTUAL HAPPINESS

Happiness is both the aim and the justification:

Of those born in this realm of desire
Both male and female desire the opposite sex.
The happiness of desire is the best of happinesses.
High and low can find it easily.

The promotion of happiness with a mate who has been brought to oneself by past karma is extolled as the best of moral behavior:

Association with a mate—brought to one by the power of previous actions (*karma*)—with love like that for one's own dear life and with abandonment of intrigues and adultery is the best of ethics.

Reflecting the Hindu division of life into phases of duty, passion, wealth, and liberation and contradicting the Buddhist emphasis on cloistered retreat even in youth, he suggests that restrictive practice of religion can be delayed to old age:

When the faculties have dulled and the mind has become peaceful, if men and women who have become gray-haired make effort at the path of religion in a place of solitude, that is the excellent behavior of earlier times. Therefore, as long as one has the wild horse of the senses and has the power of entering to the place of passion, though one partakes of the pleasures of passion, how could an intelligent being find fault!

Even more provocatively, he again mixes the secular and the sacred, suggesting that liberation—a term reserved for freedom from the entire process of cyclic existence—can be found in the home through work, faithfulness, discipline, and friendship:

Living by one's own labor in accordance with
    good teaching,
Always doing it only with one's own wife, con-
    trolling the senses,
And having a good time with friends who hap-
    pen to arrive,
An excellent being has liberation in the home.

As scandalous as the conflation of religion with worldly activities is, Gedün Chöpel provides a secular adaptation of high Buddhist ideals—much needed in a culture oriented to states beyond the reach of most practitioners.

His repeated and heartfelt advice is to have loving concern for companions out of respect based on recognizing the importance others' feelings.

As much passion as there is, there are tears, and as much attention as there is, there is expression. If by those two the fences of embarrassment are crossed, the nature of pleasure becomes very powerful. Do the deed of passion in the ways that you like it in all its forms, and taste all the forms of pleasure described in the various commentaries. When both become intoxicated with strong passion due to being well acquainted, trusting, and without qualms, during sex do not refrain from anything; do everything without exception. Those who have secret uncommon meetings unsuitable to be seen by a third party or heard by a fifth ear become the best of bosom friends in the world.

Other-concern is at the heart of his ethic of love and the *raison d'être* for the sixty-four arts of passion.

7 Enhancing Female Pleasure

Gedün Chöpel's concern that men not just act out their desires on women but respect their partners and seek to foster mutual enjoyment evinces itself in prescriptions for both men and women. He warns men not to abuse young girls:

> Forcibly doing it with a young girl produces severe pains and wounds her genitalia; consequently, later when giving birth she has difficulties. If it is not the time and if copulating would be dangerous for her, churn about between her thighs, and it will come out. In many areas it is customary to do so; it quickly promotes a girl's maturation.

Males need to know that they can help females make their genitalia ready for penetration:

> Having covered with ointment the outside of a wound up cloth, make a fine, soft point. Every day raise passion [by tickling the labia]; then put it just into the vagina. Finally the phallus should

enter. When a girl has matured, apply butter to the penis and slowly insert it. If the phallus is churned about between the thighs, the vagina naturally gets better and ripens.

Males and females need to recognize differences in their processes of arousal and what regions to stimulate:

As an example, the Sho-mang[1] plant, which is soft and shriveled, when it is soaked by water becomes hard and swells up. Just so, when drops of blood collect together, the male and female organs erect and swell. When bliss is generated in the private parts, the mind's attention goes to that spot; by that cause, the vital winds [i.e., energies] and the blood gather, filling the middle of the male member whereupon the phallus erects.

The passion of a man is light and easy to rouse; the passion of a woman is deep and hard to rouse. Therefore, if one needs purposely to raise the passion of a woman by various methods of passion, it is said that the labia and the inner nerves, the skin of the right and left sides of the mouth of the vagina, the mouth of the womb, and the points of the breasts rise and swell when passion is generated. For men the whole phallus, the pubic region, and hairy places have the feeling of bliss when passion is generated. An essential nerve is in the front of the phallus.

Having indicated that the hard-to-arouse passion of women sometimes requires additional stimulation, he emphasizes that once aroused, the entire female body can become a tender, sexual organ:

Still, the bliss of women is greatly spread out and

---

[1] Identified by Sarat Chandra Das, *A Tibetan-English Dictionary* (Calcutta, 1902), 1245, as a medicinal plant that clears away scars.

unidentifiable. They have bliss everywhere beneath the navel, the top of the thighs, the inside
of the vagina, the door of the womb, the anus,
and the area around the buttocks. In short, all the
inside and outside of the lower parts of a woman's body are pervaded by bliss, and as she can
feel such bliss, it is said that the entire body of a
woman is the feminine organ.

Because of slower arousal and yet ultimate intensity,
women require a longer period of fore-play and of copulation:

On every occasion of copulation women have the
final bliss. When a couple copulates several times,
the first time the regenerative fluid of the male is
emitted quickly, and the male has more powerful
passion. However, women are the opposite; it is
said that the first time their passion is of little
force, and the later times it increases. Therefore,
men who do not emit their regenerative fluid for
a long time and whose phallic power does not
diminish quickly give the female the glories of
passion. This is what groups of women say inside
the home.

It is said that the way the bliss of a woman is
consummated is similar to how satisfaction is
produced when itching arises in the body and a
finger scratches the spot. However, it is widely
known that during copulation a woman has bliss
even more than seven times greater than a man.
When the regenerative fluid has come out, the
man's bliss is finished; when the itch of passion is
cleared away, the woman's bliss is finished.
Therefore, if the passionate deed is done many
times, it is very consuming for the body of the
man, but it does not similarly harm the body of
the woman. Because the vagina and the labia are

uncovered naked flesh, the pleasure and pain of
women are extremely great, like touching the
mouth of a wound.

Despite the similarities between male and female genitalia mentioned earlier, the differences are also profound:

One is an external sense organ.
The other is an internal hole of the body.
As red flesh and sinews are different,
How could the thorn know the feeling of a
wound!

Males, therefore, need to know that quick sex has little
meaning to women:

By the husband's being too fast, it is said a
woman will not experience sexual pleasure even
once in three years. It would be good for a man
who does not know thus the inner experience of
his wife and life-long friend to be a hermit!

Males should both delay emission and perform the deed
multiple times:

If the man is quick, the first copulation does not
produce satisfaction in the woman. Thus those
with power and much regenerative fluid should
do it two or three times. Otherwise, when the regenerative fluid is about to come out, desist from
movement and spread out the pleasure; again
when passion rises, do it. Still, it is said that whatever is done, two times are needed.

After emission, the male should not just pull out but let
the female use the occasion of insertion to bring about
orgasm, and if she is not successful, the male should use
his fingers:

Immediately after the regenerative fluid has been

emitted, the male member should not be taken out; keep it deep in the vagina. Let her shake and move as she wants in order to consummate her pleasure. If her pleasure still is not complete, the man should enter two fingers in her vagina and stir.

Manipulation is also helpful prior to penetration. Using either his fingers or a dildo, penetration should not occur prior to the female's arousal:

In general, before copulation it is essential that with two fingers he rubs and caresses the hole of the vagina. In addition, at the beginning rub again and again the inside of the reproductive organ with a male member made of wood, and when the woman becomes aroused, do the deed.

Gedün Chöpel encourages couples to overcome any hesitancy to use a dildo by realizing that the custom is widespread:

In the southern regions this custom is still performed. When the husband goes away, the women do it to themselves. It is said that the rich will have one made even of gold, silver, brass, or the like. In India most women only know their own husbands, and as sex that fulfills expectations is rare, this custom of secrecy is very prevalent. Similarly, harems protected by eunuchs always resort to this. Stories of this have risen in our country, and in the *Kāma Sūtra* it is given as advice.[1]

He advises women who want to experience the full power of pleasure to take the lead:

The hearts of both vibrate with passion; they

---

[1] See, for instance, *Kāma Sūtra* II.6.6 and VII.2.

look with flush faces free from shame. She pulls the jewel of the organ [i.e., the head of the phallus] with her hand and enters it into the hole of her vagina. Entering only the tip, she takes it out again and again. She sends in half; again and again she takes it out. Finally she puts it all the way in and aims it upward for a long time.

With her legs pulled up, she pushes the man's buttocks [with her feet]. Her knees touch under his arm pits, and with her thighs and calves she binds and rubs downward.

Sometimes when the phallus comes out, the woman holds it with her hand and shakes it; again she rolls it between her first three fingers and sends it in. When it completely disappears, she gently rocks the scrotum and squeezes well the root of the phallus with two fingers; then she rotates it inside the vagina.

Having pressed two or three times, again and again rock and wipe the tip of the phallus with a soft cloth. Through this it will become very bulbous and hard. Sometimes also wipe the door of the vagina. Keep the area around the root of the phallus moist; wipe again and again the tip and middle. Girlfriends who want to partake of powerful pleasures should learn this quintessential instruction.

And:

Then, with lust for sex especially burning, the male is to be put below. Like a fish circling a fish, from one side of a wide bed to the other they roll and switch positions while embracing each other.

With delectable detail, he calls on women to manipulate the man's phallus. This section, called "Playing with the Organ", is written from the female's point of view:

Place the right foot on the man's shoulder, show-ing clearly the breasts and vagina. With a damp palm strike the middle of your own place of re-production. Then like the mystical dagger of the occultist, always in secret with many methods, begin any and all forms of very passionate play on the flower that is the organ of manifest plea-sure.

Embracing firmly the man's neck with your left arm, kiss again and again. Stretching the right hand, take hold of the waist of the phallus and milk it like the teat of a cow.

Likewise, wrap it between the two palms; pull a little, turn it right and left. Take hold of the root, and then shaking each other, strike the thighs, lips, and teeth.

Between the two stomachs squeeze and rub the man's erect phallus. Sometimes bind it between the thighs, and rub it in the mouth-door of the vagina.

Putting the phallus between the fingers, gaze at it with extremely passionate eyes. Take a handful of the scrotum, and rub again and again the main nerves of the pubic region.

While stroking his buttocks with your hands, touch and rub with the point of the phallus the hollows of your stomach, throat, bosom, and so forth—the places where itching and passion rise. With the tips of the breasts and the tips of the fingers, touch the hole from which the seed emerges. If especially intoxicated and stirred with passion, rub that hole with the tongue and suck.

With your fingers raise itching in the area of the root [of the organ], and with your hand put the smooth jewel in. Again and again, put it in the mouth-door of the vagina. Put it half way in and take it out.

Though these activities, no doubt, also bring pleasure to the male, they are described from the viewpoint of the ever-increasing passion and enjoyment of the female. Gedün Chöpel gives copious advice on differences between male and female in regard to how orgasm is produced, but he does not fall into the hubris that somehow he has captured all the variations:

> Thus, although the way the pleasures of passion are produced in the male and female differ greatly, from one's own individual experience, one cannot say to another, "This is it."

He has taken his own advice on the limits of conceptualization.

ADVICE ON PREGNANCY

Prescriptions concerning pregnancy found in the *Treatise on Passion* concern:

- birth control
- cautions during pregnancy
- childbirth
- sex selection of offspring.

Birth control. To prevent pregnancy Gedün Chöpel advises standing and sitting copulation in which the womb is pointed downward and the woman is not bent forward:

> In short, all methods of union (1) in which the reproductive organ is pointed downward and the phallus goes under the vagina and (2) in which the waist of the woman is not bent forward are helpful for preventing pregnancy.

The same is true of copulation in which the woman lies on top of the man.

Then, when the man has ejaculated, the woman

should stand up and pound the floor with a foot and then use a douche:

> As soon as the seminal fluid has come out, the woman should rise and pound the floor with her heel. She should wash her vagina with warm water; it is the same as medicine for the prevention of pregnancy.

Conversely, if the couple seeks conception, the woman should remain in bed with her rear elevated:

> After finishing the deed, the woman should not rise immediately; she should put a pillow under her rear and sleep. Then having drunk milk and so forth, it is good for them to sleep separately on their own beds.

Cleanliness is also important for conception, as is freedom from anxiety:

> Before copulation both the male and the female should clean away all excretions and wash their sexual organs. Especially the recesses of the vagina should be cleansed; this helps conception in flawless wombs.
>
> If during union fright, anxiety, and so forth arise, harm will occur later to the womb; therefore, it is very important to have sex in a solitary place, relaxed and without any apprehension. Afterward, while the man stops his left nostril and breathes through the right, the woman should lie down on her left side and the man on his right and sleep for a while.

Cautions during pregnancy. The signs of pregnancy are described:

> It is said that the sense that all of one's insides are filled with various types of filth, loss of appetite, and the dripping of water and mucous from the

mouth are signs of having become pregnant. If a pregnant woman has strong desire for copulation, it is a sign the child dwelling in the womb is a girl.

Avoidance of copulation during pregnancy is preferable:

> Those who have just given birth, those suffering in pregnancy, those who are ill, those with great worry, and those who are very old or very young are never suitable for the deeds of passion.

If one does copulate, it should be from the side so that the womb will not be pressed:

> If copulation can be given up, it is good. If it cannot, use methods of union from the side. If the stomach is pressed or the like when the womb has filled out, the limbs of the child will degenerate. In particular, as a thumb of the child stays around the nose, there is great danger of developing a hare lip.

Similarly, postures of deep penetration should be avoided:

> The man lies down on his back and spreads his thighs. He contracts his knees strongly. The woman puts her midriff on his pubic region and puts her two feet to the right and left of the man. Leaning back on the thighs of the man, the woman does the work of entering and pulling out. With this method the phallus enters deep inside and again and again touches the door of the womb. For this reason it is prohibited for pregnant women.

Most likely for the same reason, postures of role reversal should be avoided:

When mounting on a man, if she has not seen it before, she will look surprised. However, it is good to avoid this method if the couple is seeking to have a baby or if the woman is pregnant.

A pregnant woman should avoid situations of fright:

> Then always avoid causes producing fear, like looking down deep caverns or wells.

Childbirth. Gedün Chöpel speaks briefly about how to encourage easy birthing, how to avoid blockage, and how to cause the after-birth to emerge:

> During birth, an experienced woman should be nearby. Gently rub and squeeze the abdomen downwards. Then, when the child arrives at the door of the female organ, by squeezing strongly, it will come out easily. If the baby is obstructed at the door of the womb, fumigate with the skin of a black snake. Through stretching out the two arms and shaking them, the placenta will emerge.

Sex selection of offspring. It is generally assumed in Tibetan culture that a passionate male has boys and a passionate woman has girls; however, just the opposite is the case:

> If [a couple] wishes to have a boy, the female should raise strong passion for the male. The male should imagine himself as a woman or strive at methods of slow and weak passion. Similarly, if [a couple] wishes to have a girl, the male should generate strong passion for the fe-male; the female should stay without paying at-tention, and he should strongly emit a great deal of regenerative fluid. This is the essence of an ex-tremely important essential; the child's becoming male or female depends on this. A passionate

woman gives birth to many boys; a passionate man definitely has daughters. Therefore, it is a mistake to think that if the passion of the male is more powerful, a male child will be conceived.

For this reason, a man who wants male children should choose a passionate wife:

> Whoever's wife has powerful passion, his family lineage will definitely all be boys. Therefore, those who wish to have boys should choose and take a passionate woman.

By extension, if the couple wants a boy, intercourse should commence when the female becomes strongly aroused:

> If the deed of copulation is done when the woman generates a force of passion greater than the man, the power of pleasure is maintained, and there is no doubt of conception and birth of a boy.

To insure that the female is strongly aroused, techniques that stimulate the labia and so forth should be used. Rear entry is particularly helpful:

> Because with play from the rear the labia are touched and rubbed, arousal is high; therefore, it can satisfy with passionately strong pleasure and, moreover, can especially bestow bliss on a woman. Those methods of copulation moving in from the rear are very helpful for impregnation. If she conceives during these, it is said the son born will be extraordinary.

In cases of equally strong passion, conception of a boy is likely since the female's arousal is naturally stronger:

> If both become intoxicated through strong passion, as the woman's passion is by nature

stronger, the child produced will most likely be a male. However, [the rising of their passion] must be simultaneous.

Because the man has stronger passion at the beginning, if the couple wants a male child, the man should not emit semen in the vagina during the initial copulation. He should withdraw and ejaculate outside:

> During the first copulation the man by nature has stronger passion; hence when the regenerative fluid is emitted, he should pull out and let it go on the outside of the vagina. During the second copulation the woman's passion is ignited; therefore, the seed should be emitted in the vagina. If she is impregnated with such a technique, it definitely helps toward getting a male child.

The theory that a passionate man attracts female offspring and that a passionate woman attracts male offspring is based on Buddhist descriptions of the process of rebirth. The fourth-century Indian scholar Vasubandhu makes this assertion in brief in his *Treasury of Manifest Knowledge*,[1] but the reasons why this is so are presented in detail in Highest Yoga Tantra[2] where it is explained that in ordinary rebirth, a being in the intermediate state between the last life and the new life sees its father and mother lying together. If the being is to be reborn as a male, he desires sex with the mother and wants to separate from (that is to say, get rid of) the father. If the being is to be reborn as a female, she desires sex with the father and wants to separate from (get rid of) the mother. When the being, out of wanting to

---

[1] *chos mngon pa'i mdzod, abhidharmakośa*; III.15ab and auto-commentary. Thanks to Professor Georges Dreyfus for the reference.

[2] The description is drawn from Lati Rinbochay and Jeffrey Hopkins, *Death, Intermediate State and Rebirth in Tibetan Buddhism*, pp. 59-61.

copulate, begins to embrace the one that is desired, he or she perceives only a very large version of the desired partner's sexual organ, due to which he/she becomes frustrated and angry. In the midst of desire and anger, the being of the intermediate state dies and thereupon enters the womb, and conception takes place.

Entry into the womb is by way of passing through the father's body. According to one tantric explanation, the being of the intermediate state first enters through the father's mouth or, according to another explanation, through the top of the father's head. Having entered into the father's body, the being passes through the body and emerges by way of his phallus in the mother's vagina. With the four factors necessary for rebirth— presence of the consciousness of an intermediate state being, presence of semen, presence of ovum (called blood), and a karmic connection between father, mother, and intermediate state being—complete, rebirth is taken.

Strong passion is a factor attracting an intermediate state being, and thus—if we assume heterosexual orientation—someone destined by karma to be born as a female is drawn to a passionate male and someone destined to be reborn as a male is drawn to a passionate female. Gedün Chöpel thereby debunks the macho notion that a passionate male has many sons. He adds that the traits of the parents toward whom the being in the intermediate state is sexually drawn are passed to the children:

> The mother's disposition, constitution, physical strengths, and so forth all come to the continuums of her sons. Likewise, the father's disposition, physical constitution, and so forth all definitely arise in the continuums of his daughters.

The transmission is genetic but also is environmental in the sense that strong sexual attraction causes absorption on a deep level with that parent.

SEXIST ELEMENTS

Despite unchallengable concern for women, evidenced repeatedly in the *Treatise on Passion*—remarkable in the face of male-oriented Tibetan culture—Gedün Chöpel evinces, from time to time, biases about topics such as preference for male off-spring and subordination of women. He speaks of the birth of a boy as a *summum bonum* along with fame and riches:

> Whatever woman enhances the self-arisen phal-
> lus
> With the petals of her mouth
> Pleases the great bliss-bestowing goddess.
> She will attain glory, wealth, and the supreme of
> boys.

Even more directly, he warns that if a women's passion is not aroused before ejaculation, "Though she conceives, it will only be a daughter."

He therefore advises desisting from intercourse on odd days after menstruation since girls are conceived on those days:

> If she becomes pregnant on the fifth, seventh, ninth, eleventh, thirteenth, and fifteenth days after menstruating, she will have a daughter, and hence it is suitable to avoid copulation on those days. If from sleeping with a man on the sixth, eighth, tenth, twelfth, and fourteenth days she conceives, the child born will be a boy.

A woman's place, for the most part, is the home, taking care of her husband:

> For a woman her final home is not her father's, and it is difficult for her to succeed by seeking out her own way. A lifetime friend for a woman, like

a hornless animal in a desolate valley, is a husband. In India a wife bows down to the feet of her husband every morning and, mixing the dust of his feet with a red powder, puts a mark on her forehead.

A wife should please her husband since attempting to live by her own labor will bring little success:

Her husband provides her with food, clothing, and adornments—whatever she wishes—and leads her for a whole lifetime in all actions; aside from respecting him, there is no greater doctrine for women. A woman gives up her husband and engages in charity, asceticism, and so forth, but these roots of virtue done without consent will not bring forth vast fruit. She should stay with her husband with all the aspects of beauty that accord with her protector's thought. From the depths she should mix body and mind [with those of her husband] through the various activities of passion and pleasure.

Gedün Chöpel even mentions a passage in scripture that describes offering a woman to a desirous male as a high form of charity:

It is said in the chapter on practice in the *Kālachakra Tantra* that providing a woman for someone who is desirous is the supreme of gifts. If you do not believe me, look there, and it will be evident.

His own opinion on the matter is unclear, though his amazement is conveyed by the assumption that his readers would be shocked.

As was quoted earlier, he scolds men for not valuing women but one of the reasons is that women are such good servants:

She is the goddess with a body which when seen brings pleasure. She is the field producing a good family lineage. She is the mother acting as a nurse when one is sick and a poet consoling the mind when one is sad. She is a servant who does all of the work of the household. She is a friend who protects with fun and joy for a lifetime. One's wife with whom one has become related through former actions (*karma*) is endowed with these six qualities.

Looked at from the perspective of advances toward the liberation of women in the last half of the twentieth century, Gedün Chöpel's views, as exhibited in these few passages, are wanting. However, juxtaposed with copious evidence to the contrary cited above in the section on the equality of women and men, these sexist notions are clearly in the minority and run counter to the main brunt of his presentation.

8 Classificatory Schemes

Gedün Chöpel uses a variety of schemes to classify persons in relation to sex:

- personality and size of sexual organ
- age
- ease of arousal
- facial marks
- other physical characteristics
- month of initial menstruation
- time of the month
- day in the menstrual month
- place.

PERSONALITY AND SIZE OF SEXUAL ORGAN

Based on an Indian schema put forth by Maheshvara,[1]

---

[1] In the Prologue Gedün Chöpel refers to a text by Maheshvara entitled *chags pa'i bstan bcos* (*rāgaśāstra?*). For speculation on what it may be, see Chapter Two of the Introduction.

he divides males and females into four types each[1] that are determined by personality traits and by physical characteristics. He begins with males.

Rabbit
Personality traits: good-natured, virtuous, faithful to his partner, respectful of superiors, helpful to those below him, easy-going, and lazy.

Physical characteristics: medium size body, erect penis of six finger breadths, bulbous and soft head of penis, sweet smelling sweat and seminal fluid, tends toward premature ejaculation.

Buck
Personality traits: respectful to teachers, dislikes cleaning, sharp intelligence, sings frequently, likes dressing up, is honest, throws parties for friends.

Physical characteristics: prominent eyes, large shoulders, runs and jumps when moving, little hair in armpits and public region, erect penis of eight finger breadths.

Bull
Personality traits: unstable, little social concern, gains and loses friends easily, gourmand, skilled at performing arts, copulates with all available.

Physical characteristics: large body, handsome, erect penis of ten finger breadths, bad-smelling sweat and seminal fluid.

Stallion
Personality traits: excitable, deceitful, companies with all young and old women including close relatives etc., very passionate even toward mother and sister, needs a woman every day.

---

[1] In the *Kāma Sūtra* (II.1.1-2) Vātsyāyana divides males and females into three types each; he divides males into rabbit, bull, and stallion, and females, into doe, mare, and elephant.

Physical characteristics: big, fat, rough body, dark in color, long feet, moves quickly, capable of continuous copulation, hard and thick erect penis of twelve finger breadths, copious bad-smelling seminal emission.

Sub-divisions are created by dividing each of these into four:

* rabbit-rabbit, buck-rabbit, bull-rabbit, stallion-rabbit
* buck-buck, bull-buck, stallion-buck, rabbit-buck
* bull-bull, stallion-bull, rabbit-bull, buck-bull
* stallion-stallion, rabbit-stallion, buck-stallion, bull-stallion.

Females are similarly divided into four types:[1]

Lotus
Personality traits: smiles a lot, likes clean clothes, likes simple food and natural adornments, is altruistic, virtuous, and faithful to her partner.

Physical characteristics: beautiful, slender, supple, without freckles, shiny long black hair, eyes darting about, small nostrils, thick eyebrows, soft round big breasts, vagina six finger breadths deep, menstruation fragrant like a lotus whereby this type gets its name.

Picture
Personality traits: wears colorful clothes and yellow garlands, likes pictures and stories, keeps small birds, is liked by children, and is not particularly attracted to sexual pleasure.

Physical characteristics: medium height and weight, roving long eyes, roundish genitalia, vagina eight finger breadths deep, little pubic hair, clear menstruation, and pretty as a picture whereby this type gets its name.

---

[1] This fourfold division is found at the beginning of Kokkoka's *Ratirahasya* and Kalyāṇamalla's *Anaṅgaranga*, but the details differ.

Large Conch

Personality traits: frequently eats various foods, is skilled at keeping the household as well as servants and acquaintances, talkative, clear mind, slightly secretive, acquaints easily, has little respect for elders, mixes well with family, very jealous, and passionate.

Physical characteristics: tall and thin with a crooked neck, nose points upward, long face of beautiful color, warm genitalia, vagina ten finger breadths deep, thick pubic hair, secretes easily, sour-smelling sweat and vagina.

Elephant

Personality traits: eats a lot, strong and anxious voice, covers body with adornments, likes adultery and gos-sip, divorces her partner, likes big strong men and any-one else, wants to sleep with even father and son, wants to copulate multiple times each day, insatiable.

Physical characteristics: short in stature with broad limbs and large hips, rounded shoulders, thick mouth and nose, very large and hard breasts, and a very hairy pubic region burning with heat and dripping with secretion that smells like an elephant whereby this type gets its name.

Again, sub-divisions are created by dividing each of these into four:

- lotus-lotus, picture-lotus, conch-lotus, elephant-lotus
- picture-picture, conch-picture, elephant-picture, lotus-picture
- conch-conch, elephant-conch, lotus-conch, picture-conch,
- elephant-elephant, lotus-elephant, picture-elephant, conch-elephant.

Woman of the four types are to be courted in different environments. For a woman of the lotus type:

Prepare a atmosphere of peace: cover soft cushions with a white cloth; place vessels of fragrant waters nearby; and arrange bunches of small flowers.

Picture:

Prepare an atmosphere of beauty: cover a bouncy bed with a multicolored cloth; also arrange various pictures; and place edibles like honey and so forth nearby.

Conch:

Prepare an atmosphere of wealth: cover the bed with deer skin, smooth and supple; surround it with cushions of various sizes; and place lovely sounding musical instruments there.

Elephant:

Play in an atmosphere of power: place a hard mattress with thin cushions on a bed surrounded by darkness; and nearby place foods that are aphrodisiacs, like the meat of fish.

AGE

Gedün Chöpel divides women into four classes based on stage of life.[1] He names the first three—juvenile, youth, and mature woman:

A female who is twelve years and younger is called a juvenile. She should be given combs, honey, pastries, etc. She should be told stories of the pleasures of kissing.

From thirteen through twenty-five she is called a youth; she should be kissed and pinched.

---

[1] Although in chapter four of Kokkoka's *Ratirahasya* and Kalyāṇamalla's *Anaṅgaranga* females are divided into four classes by age, the ages are not the same as in this list.

> Getting acquainted with men, she will experience joy.
> From twenty-six through fifty she is a mature woman. She should be told stories of passion and bitten and pinched and likewise should be given the enjoyment of passion.
> A woman over fifty should be respected with pleasant and honorific words. Her good advice should be asked for both the short- and long-term.

Since males mature later, he prescribes different ages of males and females for marriage:

> A male at the age of sixteen is pubescent and at age twenty-four is complete. A female at the age of thirteen is pubescent and at the age of sixteen is complete. Therefore, a male of twenty-four years and a woman of sixteen or eighteen are at a time suitable for sex. They may keep a home from that age.

Because of their respective ages of sexual maturity, early sexual activity has different effects on males and females—wearing out males and maturing females. Gedün Chöpel defensively explains that, as a man, he did not just make this up to satisfy a desire for young women:

> If one waits for a long time beyond those years, it is said various illnesses will arise. If at a young age men do it with women, they will lose their power and will age quickly. However, if women meet with men at a young age, it is said they thereby forestall aging. This is not something that I made up; I am explaining what has been proven by the experience of old men and women.

EASE OF AROUSAL

Women are divided into two types, based on whether sexual arousal is hard or easy. The former are called "hard", and the latter, "dripping":

> Thus led on the path of manifest intoxication by various arts of passion, the two types of women, hard and dripping, should proceed on the path of pleasure in accordance with their wishes. Not changing in body and mind and difficult to raise her passion, this type of woman is known as hard. Quickly changing composure and generating the moisture of the feminine secretion, this type is known as dripping.

For the hard and the dripping, from among the many postures described earlier Gedün Chöpel singles out one each :

> The woman puts her thighs together and forcefully stretches out her legs. The man climbs on like a frog. He pushes hard with his phallus like a mystical dagger. This is called very powerful, *hula*, and should be done especially for the hard type.

And:

> Sometimes take hold of the root of the phallus with a hand and move it around inside the vagina. It is medicine to clear away the pangs of passion; it should especially be done to the dripping type.

FACIAL MARKS

A list of nineteen varieties of moles on the face, neck, breasts, and shoulders is given for the sake of predicting the future for both women and men. Described by the author as unreliable, they are near the end of Chapter One of the translation.

OTHER PHYSICAL CHARACTERISTICS

In Chapter Seventeen other divisions of women are determined by the placement of the vagina. For the high type, methods of front copulation are preferable; for the low type, methods of rear copulation. Through other attributes women are divided into those whose vaginas are produced from water, produced from mud, and grown from dry earth. Other physical attributes (see the Translation) serve as signs of varying degrees of passion. The author seems to have collected this material from Indian sources but without any particular interest.

MONTH OF INITIAL MENSTRUATION

In Chapter Three the month in the lunar calendar when a girl initially menstruates is used as a means to predict her future in terms of wealth, respect, virtue, courage, education, health, fate of her children, intelligence, and so forth.

TIME OF THE MONTH

Gedün Chöpel repeats an Indian theory that an essential physical fluid moves about the body in accordance with the phase of the moon and thus sexual arousal can be enhanced through stimulating those erogenous zones in accordance with the date of the lunar month. This notion is found in the second chapter of Kokkoka's *Ratirahasya* but not in the *Kāma Sūtra*. The centers of sexual excitement—ranging from the top of the head to the feet— become more active on certain days of the lunar month, and thus are more prone to stimulation:

Moreover, because the physical essence moves about the places of the body day by day, it is said that if those places are kissed and so forth at certain times, passion increases greatly. From dawn until twelve midnight on the sixteenth day [of the lunar month] the essence stays at the top of the head. Similarly, on the seventeenth it is at the ears, and on the eighteenth, at the nose. Then from the nineteenth until the end of the month day by day it moves to the mouth, cheeks, shoulders, chest, stomach, navel, waist, pubic region, thighs, knees, calves, and upper part of the feet. Again, on the first of the month it is at the calves, and the second, the knees; on the third likewise it is at the thighs. Similarly apply the remaining body-parts to the days until the fifteenth, when it pervades the whole body.

DAY IN THE MENSTRUAL MONTH

Gedün Chöpel relates Indian prescriptions for and prohibitions against copulation on certain days of the menstrual month. As was mentioned earlier, copulation on odd days after menstruation leads to conception of female offspring, whereas copulation on even days leads to conception of male offspring. For the specific qualities of the children conceived on those days, see Chapter Seventeen. Gedün Chöpel relates a general fertility theory:

Many scholars have said that most of the fruits of timeliness are just inevitable. In particular, from the cessation of menstruation to the eighth day afterward, the mouth of the womb is open, due to which conception is definite. Though conception could occur after the eighth day, with most women the door of the womb has closed.

Gedün Chöpel warns men that it is their duty to satisfy the sexual needs of their mates:

A woman's craving for sex is very strong for two or three months after conceiving. It is also very strong when, after giving birth, the purificatory rites have been performed and she is free from sickness and also when a day has passed after finishing menstruation. If while the man is nearby he does not do it with his wife, he will go to a fearful hell upon dying since he abandons the better teachings of behavior for men.

PLACE

In Chapter Five, Gedün Chöpel conveys a sense of the immense variety of sexual expression through relating hearsay about women in various areas of India. Based mostly on the *Kāma Sūtra*, the descriptions revolve around what sexual arts are most stimulating for them, how passionate they are, their physical characteristics, how easy they are, pretensions, inhibitions, disposition for multiple partners, and so forth.

In Chapter Four, he speaks of women whose clitoris is so large they can even do the deed with another woman. He also speaks of natural transsexuals:

Some of the type who have a large clitoris have both sex signs or change back and forth from one to the other. There are a great many women who, from a little change in physique, have become males. Similarly, it is well known that some men whose penis retracts greatly inside have become women.[1]

---

[1] For more on this topic see Leonard Zwilling, "Homosexuality as Seen in Indian Buddhist Texts" in *Buddhism, Sexuality, and Gender*, edited by José Ignacio Cabezón, 206.

About Western women he says:

> In general a girl of the West is beautiful, splendorous, and more courageous than others. Her behavior is coarse, and her face is like a man's. There is even hair around her mouth. Fearless and terrifying, she can be tamed only by passion. Able to suck the phallus at the time of play, the girl of the West is known to drink the regenerative fluid. She does it even with dogs, bulls, and any other animals and with father and son, etc. She goes without hesitation with whoever can give the enjoyment of sex.

It seems that the reputation of Western women as known in India in the late 1930's was based, at least in part, on imported pornography.

* * *

These seven themes—equality of women, sixty-four arts of love, sexual pleasure and spiritual insight, a mutually supportive ethic of love, increasing female sexual pleasure, pregnancy, and classificatory schemes—are interwoven throughout Gedün Chöpel's *Treatise on Passion*. The book is more evocative and more accessible than the three most popular erotic texts of India—the third-century *Kāma Sūtra* by Vātsyāyana, the ninth- or tenth-century *Ratirahasya* by Kokkoka, and the sixteenth-century *Anaṅgaranga* by Kalyāṇamalla.

The *Kāma Sūtra* is the principal source for all subsequent Indian erotica (although the *Ratirahasya*, for instance, includes other material), and it is also the principal source for Gedün Chöpel's *Treatise on Passion*. His presentation, like many of the post-Vātsyāyana Indian texts, focuses on the eight forms of sexual union—embracing, kissing, pinching and scratching, biting, moving to and fro and pressing, making erotic noises, role reversal, and ways of copulating—which are found in the second section of the *Kāma Sūtra*; thus, it does not treat many topics of the other six parts of the *Kāma Sūtra* such as acquisition of a girl for marriage, the rights and duties of an ideal wife, extra-marital sex, the ways of courtesans, and potions, etc., for seduction. In a sense, Gedün Chöpel's text gets to the heart of the matter with deliciously evocative descriptions of sexual acts and titillatingly inviting advice to shun inhibitions, creatively expanding on his sources.

From among the other themes, Gedün Chöpel's presentation of classificatory schemes is clearly Indian although not completely corresponding to the above-mentioned three texts. The advice on pregnancy seems to be a mixture of Indian and Tibetan origin. The techniques for increasing female sexual pleasure, even if based on Indian sources, achieve a new prominence in Gedün Chöpel's work, which, unlike his Indian predecessors, is not concerned with gaining and controlling women but with enhancing the quality of their sexual experience. Thus, I find the theme of the equality of women to be his own contribution.

Also, unlike the Indian texts, Gedün Chöpel weaves the Indo-Tibetan tantric perspective of spiritual sexual union into his general treatise on the arts of secular love such that an underlying and over-arching focus is sexual ecstasy as a door to spiritual experience of the fundamental state. Because of his conviction in the inter-penetration of the worldly and the spiritual, the religious focus, however, does not turn the material on sexual acts into metaphor for union with the divine—which would be a denial of physical sex. Rather, ordinary sex is viewed as a basis for possible development into extraordinary insight. The sky-experience of the mind of clear light impinges into and stands behind his scintillating descriptions of erotic acts, beckoning the reader to taste reality.

Kāma Shāstra

TREATISE ON PASSION

by Gedün Chöpel

Editions of the Text

As Gedün Chöpel says in the colophon, he finished the manuscript of the *Treatise on Passion* (*'dod pa'i bstan bcos*) in 1938 while staying "in the home of Gangā Deva from Pañcāla, friend with the same life-style" in the city of Mathurā, India. The manuscript was conveyed to an aristocrat in the government, Ḡap-shö Chö-gyel-nyi-ma.[1] The manuscript was circulated in Hla-śa until its first publication in Delhi in 1967 by T. G. Dhongthog[2] Rinpoche with a brief preface. That edition of 127 pages was based on a copy of the manuscript by M. J. Driver which was in the possession of Du-jom Rin-ḅo-chay,[3] then head of the Ñying-ma-ḅa order.

The 1967 edition is replete with errors, probably due to the fact that it was based on a copy of the original manuscript and not the original itself. In 1969 T. G. Dhongthog Rinpoche published a second edition in 100 pages in Delhi with extensive editing together with the *Treatise on Passion: Treasure Pleasing All the World*[4] by Ju Mi-pam-gya-tso[5] (1846-1912) and a new short preface. This edition also is based on a copy of the original, but the editing resolves many problems in the 1967 edition. The 1969 edition minus the preface was reprinted by the Tibetan Cultural Printing Press in Dharamsala, India, in 1983.

The entire text, except for occasional interlinear notes, is written in a clear and comprehensible style in poetry with seven syllables per line. I have rendered most of the text in prose but have occasionally used free verse when the content is more inspired.

---

[1] *ka shod chos rgyal nyi ma*; born 1903. See Stoddard, 330.

[2] *gdong thog/ bstan pa'i rgyal mtshan.*

[3] *bdud 'joms rin po che*; 1904-1987. This is according to Stoddard, 330. Du-jom Rin-ḅo-chay furnished the ink and paper to Da-wa-sang-ḅo to compile Gedün Chöpel's *Ornament for the Thought of Nāgārjuna*.

[4] *'dod pa'i bstan bcos 'jig rten kun tu dga' ba'i gter.*

[5] *'ju mi pham rgya mtsho/mi pham 'jam dbyangs rnam rgyal.*

Prologue

Homage to the Buddhas.

May you be protected by the self-arisen Great
Seal[1]
Rolling into one all stable and moving things
With the lightning lasso of immutable adaman-
tine pleasure
Gone to the one hundred and eight limits.

Obeisance to the feet of Maheshvara
Whose appealing body has the cast of the stain-
less sky,
Who eternally plays in the glory of pleasure
without emission,
And who resides on the snowy Mount Kailāsa[2] of
Tibet.

I bow down to the feet of the goddess Gaurī,[3]

---

[1] *phyag rgya chen po, mahāmudrā.*

[2] *ti se.*

[3] She is also known as Durgā and Pārvatī.

167

Whose beautiful face has the cast of the full
  moon,
Whose smiling white teeth are like a pearl rosary,
Whose swelling breasts have the form of a bulbous conch.[1]

This realm of passion is on the level of passion in which
all beings seek passion. The fulfillment of all enjoyments
of passion is just the passionate bliss of the union of
male and female organs. Who is the man that does not
desire a woman? Who is the woman that does not desire a man? Except for the difference of external pretension, all definitely like it.

In the *Aṅguttara*[2] *Sūtra* of Sri Lanka, the following
was spoken from the mouth of the Buddha Bhagavat:

The finality of beauty of form in the eye of a man
is the body of a woman; in the eye of a woman,
the body of a man. A beauty exceeding this I
have not seen. Among sounds the finality of
melodiousness to the ear of a man is the voice of
a woman; to the ear of a woman, the voice of a
man. There is nothing more melodious exceeding
this.

He likewise spoke about the other three sensual pleasures—smell, taste, and touch.

Many thousands of years before Buddha appeared in
the world, there were in India many sūtras and treatises
of the Brahmanical system. These were the *Sūtra for
Householders*,[3] the *Sūtra for Those Who Have Left the
Household*,[4] the *Sūtra of Passion*,[5] and so forth. The ways

---

[1] That is to say, the bulbous part of a conch.

[2] The 1983 edition (5.17) reads *uṅgu ta ra*; the 1967 edition (2.5) reads
aṅgu ta ra.

[3] *khyim gyi mdo, gṛhyasūtra.*

[4] *rab tu byung ba'i mdo.*

[5] *'dod pa'i mdo, kāmasūtra.*

of going and living of those ordained and those living in households were explained by the great sages of the past. All the customs of India come from those. One of the eighteen topics of science mentioned in some sūtras is just these methods of sex. In the *Extensive Sport Sūtra*,[1] in a list of qualities suitable for being the queen of a Bodhisattva, "Knowing the treatises like a prostitute" is given; this is taken as meaning that she must know the ways of sex. In other works also, "A woman who knows the treatises" is mentioned; in those, too, the "treatises" are said to be the ways of sex. The *Brief Treatise on Passion*[2] composed by the master Surūpa[3] was translated into Tibetan. There is a treatise called *The Play of Pleasure*[4] by the brahmin scholar Koka, son of the Kashmiri king Paribhadra;[5] though it was not translated into Tibetan, scattered parts of an Indian edition are in Ngor Monastery.[6] It is reported that there also is a treatise by Nāgārjuna.

---

[1] *rgya cher rol pa, lalitavistara*; P763, vol. 27.

[2] *'dod pa'i bstan bcos nyung ngu*. In the Peking edition (P3323, vol. 157, 31.5.2-33.1.1) the title of the text is merely *Treatise on Passion* (*'dod pa'i bstan bcos*), but in the colophon the author calls it *Condensed Treatise on Passion* (*'dod pa'i bstan bcos bsdus pa*), and thus I take Gedün Chöpel's "brief" (*nyung ngu*), which is similar to "condensed" (*bsdus pa*), to be part of the title. Otherwise, the phrase should be translated as "brief *Treatise on Passion*".

[3] *gzugs bzang zhabs*.

[4] *dga' ba'i rol pa*. Koka, or Kokkoka (Moti Chandra, 54-56), is well known for his *Secrets of Pleasure* (*ratirahasya*) which Gedün Chöpel lists below as *dga' ba'i gsang ba*. According to Richard Burton in his Introduction to the *Anandaranga* (23), the *Ratirahasya* is also known as the *Līlaśāstra*, and thus since a separate work by Kokkoka is not known, the *dga' ba'i rol pa* (which in Sanskrit would be *ratilīla*) and *dga' ba'i gsang ba* (*ratirahasya*) are the same.

[5] *zhi ba'i blon*. Moti Chandra (55) gives his father's name as "Paribhadra alias Gadya Vidyadhara Kavi", and thus I have rendered the Tibetan name as Paribhadra.

[6] Located in Dzang Province (*gtsang*), near Shi-ga-dzay (*gzhi ka rtse*).

Sūtras and treatises on passion widely renowned in India nowadays are *The Crest Jewel of the Gods of Passion* (*kandarpacuḍāmaṇi*),[1] *Form of the Bodiless One* (*anaṅgaraṅga*),[2] *The Arts of Passion* (*kāmakalā*),[3] *The Secrets of Pleasure* (*ratirahasya*),[4] *The Jeweled Lamp of Pleasure* (*ratiratnapradīpikā*),[5] *Five Arrows* (*pañcasāyaka*),[6] and so forth. Putting together the large and the small, there are over thirty. The best among them are the *Treatise on Desire*[7] by Maheshvara and the *Sūtra on Passion*[8] by Vātsyāyana.[9] Here I will explicate the arts of passion in reliance on those.

---

[1] *'dod lha'i gtsug nor*. Gedün Chöpel provides the Sanskrit of the titles of these six texts.

[2] *lus med yan lag*.

[3] *'dod pa'i sgyu rtsal*.

[4] *dga'i ba'i gsang ba*.

[5] *dga'i ba'i rin chen rnam gsal*.

[6] *mda' lnga pa*.

[7] *chags pa'i bstan bcos*. For speculation on what this text may be, see Chapter Two of the Introduction.

[8] *'dod pa'i mdo, kāmasūtra*.

[9] The 1983 edition (7.14) reads *bar pa ya na*; the 1967 edition (4.12) reads *bar sa ya na*.

1 Types of Men and Women

MALES

Though there are many types of males, there are none that are not included in these four types—rabbit, buck, bull, and stallion. The rabbit type has medium-sized body; his thoughts are good and his face smiling. He is a doer of virtue and mixes with good friends. He has abandoned cohabiting with others' wives. He respects those above him and helps those below. He eats and wears what can be attained easily. He does not worry about the past and the future; always lazy, he stays playfully happy. His masculine member when erect is about six finger breadths. The shape of his jewel [head of penis] is bulbous and soft. He copulates quickly and his seminal fluid is ejected quickly. His sweat and seminal fluid smell pleasantly. There are many of the rabbit type in good and comfortable areas.

The buck type has prominent eyes and large shoulders. He respects his teachers and does not like the

171

work of cleaning. His intelligence is sharp, and when he moves, he runs and jumps. He is always singing; he wears good adornments and clothes. He speaks truthfully, and his appetite is big. He always gives food and parties to his friends. He has little hair in the pubic region and the arm pits. His penis is about eight finger breadths long. In almost all of the countries on earth there are many men of the buck type.

The bull type has a big body and handsome countenance. His nature is unstable, and he has little embarrassment. It is easy for him to make friends, and it is easy for him to split from them. He eats a great deal and is skillful at singing and dancing. His behavior is wayward, and his passion great. He does it with all the women he can find. His phallus is about ten finger breadths long. His sweat and seminal fluid have a bad smell. Mostly in areas on the shores of oceans and in areas with great plains there are many of the bull type.

The stallion type is fat, and his body rough and big. His color is blackish; his feet are long, and he moves quickly. He is excitable; he likes deceit and falsehood. He keeps company with all women, young and old. This type is extremely passionate. If they would agree, he would do it with even his mother and sister. He goes with all the unsuitable—close relatives, daughters of clergy, and so forth. However much he copulates, his strength is not lost. It is difficult for him to stay even one day without a woman. His phallus is hard and very thick; when erect, it is about twelve finger breadths. His seminal fluid is considerable and has a bad smell. In all countries there are many of this type, but there are many more in rough, hot regions of little rain and water.

If the four fundamental types described this way are again divided more extensively, there are sixteen types. For example, there are the rabbit of the rabbit type, the buck of the rabbit type, the bull of the rabbit type, and the stallion of the rabbit type. Similarly, the buck type has four, and the bull type and stallion type also each have four. The subtle differences of these types are understood by the wise when they analyze in detail.

FEMALES

Though there are many types of females, there are none that are not included into these four types—lotus, picture, large conch, and elephant. A woman of the lotus type is the best. She is beautiful, with smiling face; her body is slender and supple. She has no freckles, and her color is ruddy and white. She has shiny very long black hair, and her eyes move about like a frightened deer. Her nostrils are small; her eyebrows are thick. She likes clean clothes and simple food. She wears only a few adornments, like flowers and so forth. She is altruistic and a doer of virtue. She has abandoned desire for other than her own husband. Her breasts are soft, round, and big. Her vagina is about six finger breadths deep. Her menstruation emits a fragrance like a lotus; therefore she is of the lotus type. The wife of King Rāma,[1] Sītā,[2] and the wife of the Pāṇḍava[3] [princes], Draupadī, and so forth are lotus types. Mostly in former times there were many of the lotus type; they are born among good lineages in the central areas of agreeable lands.

The picture type is of medium height. She is not very fat and not very thin. She has roving long eyes which are like the petals of a lotus. Her nose is like the sesame flower. She wears clothes of various colors and a garland of yellow flowers. She likes all kinds of pictures.

---

[1] *dga' byed*.

[2] *rol rnyed ma*. Sītā is the heroine of the *Rāmāyaṇa*.

[3] *skya sangs bu lnga*. These are the five brothers, sons of Paṇḍu, who shared Draupadī as their common wife. See the *Mahābhārata*.

She is enthusiastic to hear interesting stories. She keeps various small birds, parrots, and so forth. Always a group of children stays around her. Her body is as beautiful as a painted picture; therefore she is said to be of the picture type. She has less inclination for the bliss of copulation. Her other attributes are like those of the lotus type. Her reproductive organ is roundish and eight finger breadths deep. Her pubic area has little hair, and her menstruation is clear. Ulomakā and Rasajñā[1] are women of the picture type. It is said that the picture type appear on the banks of great rivers, such as the Ganges, Kaveri, and Sindhu [Indus].

The large conch type is thin and tall. Her neck is crooked; the tip of her nose goes upward. The shape of her face is long and of beautiful color. She eats various foods again and again. She is clever at protecting her household, her servants, and those around her. She talks well; her mind is clear, and she is only a little secretive. It is easy for her to become acquainted quickly with all whom she meets. She has little respect for her elders, but it is said she mixes compatibly with her own family. Her jealousy and passion are great. Her genitals are warm and ten finger breadths deep. Her pubic hair is thick, and her secretion comes out easily. A sour odor is emitted from her body and vagina. Most women of the world are included in the great conch type but from differences of the quality and temperature of the region many different shapes and colors occur. The three qualities of being talkative, having a facile tongue, and having a crook in the neck are taken as being unmistakable signs of this type.

The elephant type is short; her limbs are broad. Her mouth and nose are thick. Her hips are larger than anything else. Her eyes are reddish; her hair, coarse; her shoulders, rounded. Her breasts are very large and

---

[1] *ro ldan ma.*

hard like stone. She eats a great deal, and her voice is strong and anxious. She covers her whole body from head to foot with adornments. She likes adultery and low gossip. Most of this type separate from their hus-bands. She acquaints with large men of great strength and with all others she finds. As she has strong passion burning hard, she wants to sleep with even son and fa-ther. She needs to copulate many times each day. Though a hundred men do it, she is not satisfied. Her genitalia is very hairy and burns with heat like fire. It is always dripping wet and has an odor like that of an ele-phant. An adulteress like her is not suitable as a wife, but as she is vigorous in the act, she is renowned as the superior of maid servants.

By dividing again each of the four fundamental types of women into four, there are sixteen types. Understand the divisions—the lotus of lotus type, etc.—in accor-dance with what was explained earlier about the types of men.

These divisions were spoken by Maheshvara.[1] Vātsyāyana[2] speaks of two groups of three types each, making six. In that system the three types of males are rabbit, buck, and stallion. The three types of females are doe, mare, and elephant. The best, middle, and last of those two groups should be understood according to the order of their presentation. Though many modes of division are explained in the commentaries, except for only minor points they all agree.

MARKS

If a woman has a red mole at the root of her left cheek,

---

[1] In his Introduction Gedün Chöpel refers to a text by Maheshvara entitled *chags pa'i bstan bcos* (*rāgaśāstra?*). For speculation on what it may be see Chapter Two of the Introduction.

[2] *Kāma Sūtra*, II.1.1-2.

though she undergoes difficulties and suffering in her youth, after age thirty she will attain happiness, comfort, and glory. If the mole is black, after the age forty she will become happy.

Whoever has a black mole at the hairline in the middle of the forehead has a bad nature and will not be compatible with friends. If it is red, her husband will love her.

If she has a mole on the left side of her forehead, all will love her and she will find wealth and respect.

If she has a mole on the right side of the forehead, none of the activities that she begins will reach conclusion.

If she has a series of greenish moles beneath her left eye brow, she will encounter extensive resources, and her ethical behavior being good, her husband will love her.

If she has a red mole at the corner of an eye, she will suffer without interruption and will die by knife or sword.

If she has moles on her cheek bones, she will be neither very rich nor very poor.

Whoever has a mole on her nose will go to faraway areas, and whatever she begins will be accomplished.

If she has a mole on the back part of the right cheek, it is said she will undergo acute suffering.

Whoever has a mole in the area around the mouth will be loved by all and will find enjoyment of food and wealth.

If she has a mole in the middle of her neck, she will without doubt become wealthy.

If she has a mole inside an ear, it is said she is energetic and all persons respect her.

If she has a mole on her neck, she will gain resources from an unexpected direction.

If she has a mole on her left breast, she will give birth to many girls, and she will suffer.

It is said that whatever woman has a mole on her right breast will give birth to many boys.

If she has moles on both shoulders, she will have great power such that it will be difficult for any to sup-press her.

If she has a mole on her chest, her thought is bad. If she has a mole on her abdomen, her appetite is great.

Whatever marks of virtue or fault have been explained with respect to the left side of a woman's body should be applied in reverse to the right side for men. However, these are not very trustworthy.

STAGES

A female who is twelve years and younger is called a juvenile. She should be given combs, honey, pastries, etc. She should be told stories of the pleasures of kissing.

From thirteen through twenty-five she is called a youth; she should be kissed and pinched. Getting acquainted with men, she will experience joy.

From twenty-six through fifty she is a mature woman. She should be told stories of passion and bitten and pinched and likewise should be given the enjoyment of passion.

A woman over fifty should be respected with pleasant and honorific words. Her good advice should be asked for both the short- and long-term.

2 The Passionate Relationship

Of those born in this realm of desire
Both male and female desire the opposite sex.
The happiness of desire is the best of happi-
nesses.
High and low can find it easily.

If they were not joined by the relationship of copulation, the male and the female sexes would be separate.
Thus in the world there would be two parties, and they
would be certain to live in war and controversy. Monks
who live in the solitude of hermitages indeed do not
understand the value of this, but even the dependent-
arising in which a life-support with the eighteen types of
leisure and fortune is attained comes first from this. It is
said that if sex were abandoned, this world would definitely become empty in a moment. If there were no
human beings, how could there be monks and the
Buddhist teaching?

The two superior persons[1] and the six scholars who were like ornaments[2] were born in the country of India. The teacher [of Bön], Šhen-rap,[3] was born in the area of Öl-mo.[4] A Ming Emperor was born in a palace[5] in China. One does not need to explain where they actually came from.

Non-Buddhist books say that the Brahmin caste was produced from the mouth of Brahmā. This is difficult to accept as true, but no one, clever or stupid, can deny that all four castes are born from the genitals of women.

Among men and women who have lost all wealth and power, even an old man whose head is whiter than a conch experiences unspeakable pleasure in the vagina of an old woman. In passion there is no constraining or beating with bad thought and there is no stabbing with the spear of a harmful mind. Though there is no virtue in giving passion to a being of the realm of desire, from where could any sin come?

It is said in the chapter on practice in the *Kālachakra Tantra* that providing a woman for someone who is desirous is the supreme of gifts. If you do not believe me, look there, and it will be evident.

Beggars frown on gold, and hungry guests spit at food. Sex is disclaimed from the mouths of all, but it alone is what is liked from the minds of all. Only the wealthy obtain gold, silver, horses, and cattle; all, high and low, find the pleasures of sex. Precious things like the light of the sun, wind, earth, and rivers are common to all. If one thinks that everything interesting on the earth is made by humans, is there a deed of greater

---

[1] Guṇaprabha and Shākyaprabha.

[2] Nāgārjuna, Āryadeva, Asaṅga, Vasubandhu, Dignāga, and Dharmakīrti.

[3] *gshen rab.*

[4] *'ol mo.*

[5] *mkhar.*

meaning than the union of male and female? Not need-
ing the strain of earnestly being exhorted to the important deed, all men and women enter into it freely; this is
the system of law set by the king, cause and effect.
Are you not amazed at how the living statue of the
Foremost Bu-dön[1] was made through male and female
lying down for half an hour without depending on
learning crafts or science! Indeed all the magic of the
union of causes and conditions is amazing, but the
magic of the union of male and female is the most
amazing of all. That all the stupid, who do not know the
amazing subjects of study, know this naturally without
study is extremely amazing. Ša-ğya[2] Lama said that not
holding as amazing what is amazing is a sign of stupid-
ity.

Alas, I am crazy nowadays, and though those who
are not will laugh at me, the experience of bliss is not of
little meaning, and the birth of family lineages is not of
little meaning. If one can sustain the way of passion
from within bliss and emptiness, how can that have little
meaning?

For every man there is a woman, and for every
woman there is a man. In the mind of both there is desire for sex. What chance do those living with clean rules
have? By prohibiting suitable deeds in actuality and by
promoting unsuitable deeds in secrecy, how can religious and worldly morality suppress this natural passion of humans! How could it be correct to prohibit as
faulty the bliss naturally abiding in the nerve-structure
of the five chakras[3] in the vajra-city of six essences![4]

---

[1] *bu ston rin chen grub*; 1290-1364.

[2] Ša-ğya Paṇḍita (*sa skya paṇḍita*; 1182-1251).

[3] These are the channel-wheels at the top of the head, throat, heart,
navel, and base of the spine.

[4] The vajra-city is the body, and the six essences are—according to
one interpretation—earth, water, fire, wind, channels, and drops.

Taking pleasure in desirable objects is passion, but taking pleasure in desirable objects is faith itself. Fearing undesirable objects is hatred, but fearing undesirable objects is renunciation itself. Whether something is desired or not is a feature of the mind. Though one tried to change this, it could not be avoided. Therefore, when examined carefully, the usage of afflictive emotions in the path is the system of all vehicles.

For all activities whatsoever—large and small, for one's own sake, for the general good of the country, for the reign of a king, for the livelihood of beggars—what is indispensable is a woman. Whether making prayer-wishes for the sake of what is wanted or making offering to favored gods, it is said that if one works at these together with women, the effect quickly and inevitably matures.

This huge world is like a great fearful desert; by the power of many former actions beings definitely will suffer. That which is able to bestow the comforts of pleasure in such a world seems to be the magic of the deeds of a playful woman-friend. She is the goddess with a body which when seen brings pleasure. She is the field producing a good family lineage. She is the mother acting as a nurse when one is sick and a poet consoling the mind when one is sad. She is a servant who does all of the work of the household. She is a friend who protects with fun and joy for a lifetime. One's wife with whom one has become related through former actions (*karma*) is endowed with these six qualities. Hence, the claim that women are unstable and adulterous is extremely untrue.

There is no difference between men and women with

According to another interpretation, they are bone, marrow, and regenerative fluid obtained from the father, and flesh, skin, and blood obtained from the mother. See Lati Rinbochay and Jeffrey Hopkins, *Death, Intermediate State, and Rebirth in Tibetan Buddhism* (London: Rider, 1979; rpt. Ithaca: Snow Lion, 1980), 30.

regard to adultery. If one examines it carefully, men are worse. A king's having a thousand queens is still proclaimed as high-class style. If a woman has a hundred men, she is slandered as if there is nothing comparable. If [a king] does it alternately with a thousand women, where is there any sense of adultery! Since doing it with a wife is not adultery, how could the rich ever be adulterous! An old man of wealth with hair like snow selects and buys a young girl. Being a mere article sold, she is given a price. Alas, women have no protectors! When a man chooses and takes her by force, the woman has not come to him by her own wish; therefore, like trying to patch wood with stone, how could the natures of women be stable!

In the country of Persia[1] each old man takes about ten young wives, but if one wife commits adultery, she is immediately killed by being burned alive. Though one man is satisfied with five young women, how could five young women be satisfied with one old man? In that way, in many areas of the world the wealthy have many laws and customs of their own wish. This is given the name of goodness, and since it meets with the wishes of the king of the country, the skillful also show smiling approval. If one thinks about it, there is no relief from sorrow. So, do not listen just to the great noise proclaimed in one voice by beings of the same male sex; for once, witness the characteristics of the truth and speak only the honest speech of the unbiased!

For a woman her final home is not her father's, and it is difficult for her to succeed by seeking out her own way. A lifetime friend for a woman, like a hornless animal in a desolate valley, is a husband. In India a wife bows down to the feet of her husband every morning and, mixing the dust of his feet with a red powder, puts a mark on her forehead.

---

[1] *ta zig.*

In Nepal even if a man takes a woman forcibly and acts out his passion, when he finishes she rises, touches her head to his feet, and goes. First, she struggles, saying, "No," and afterwards bows saying, "Thank you." Thinking about it, one bursts out laughing; it is even said those who do so have good behavior.

Her husband provides her with food, clothing, and adornments—whatever she wishes—and leads her for a whole lifetime in all actions; aside from respecting him, there is no greater doctrine for women. A woman gives up her husband and engages in charity, asceticism, and so forth, but these roots of virtue done without consent will not bring forth vast fruit. She should stay with her husband with all the aspects of beauty that accord with her protector's thought. From the depths she should mix body and mind [with those of her husband] through the various activities of passion and pleasure.

Some men keep a mistress and then give her up. It is said that the pure gods fear to be touched even by a breeze that has scattered the dust of the feet of a woman of degenerate body and ethics; it is said the gods will run away.

Half of the body of a husband is his wife, and half of the body of a wife is her husband. With one's body split in half, it is difficult even to enter among animals. Thinking so, if one can reach the end of the lifetime having established a mind of love toward one's mate without being two-faced, even one's corpse will be an object of worship.

Giving up praising as proper that which is not, giving up the various forms of adultery, and putting a sign of copulation [a child] at the breast of a woman are the respectable ways of the world.

Though much has been said about the features that make women fit and unfit for the act,[1] it is mostly suffi-

---

[1] See, for instance, the *Kāma Sūtra* I.5.

cient to proceed according to the customs prevalent in one's own area. Indians are strongly prohibited and constrained from copulating with a widow. When this is examined with reasoning, one sees no prohibition and even sees great benefit [in having sexual relations with widows]. Therefore, widows who have finished their grief and are young are suitable for the deed.

The custom of remaining for three years without meeting any men after the death of the husband is seen in many areas. If it is possible, since the custom is very good, it should be followed.

It is said in some systems of behavior[1] that because widows are unclean, food made by them should not be eaten; however, this is a transmission of the speech of compassionless Brahmins. In ancient times in India, a woman, when her husband died, would die by jumping onto the pyre. If she could not jump onto the fire, she was considered to be a living corpse; the source of a widow's uncleanliness is only that.

The insides of the body are all only dirty; outside all beings have skin. The discrimination of humans into clean and dirty has its source in non-Buddhist systems.

Moreover, there are many explanations that relatives of the same lineage and so forth are not suitable part-ners, but other than only being customs of individual areas, it is difficult to determine in one point what is suitable and what is not. However, copulation with an-other's wife is a basis for the breaking of friendship and the arising of fights and controversy. As this is a bad, shameless deed bringing suffering in this and future lives, good people should avoid it like a contagious disease.

---

[1] Gedün Chöpel adds an interlinear note:

It is prescribed among the pledges of Devi and Vaishravana that one should not eat food, etc., from the hands of a widow.

It is explained in the *Kāma Sūtra* that it is suitable to do it with the wife of a man who has gone far away, but since the birth of a child in the not distant future brings problems like those mentioned above, it is best to avoid this. The followers of the master Bābhravya[1] say that there is no fault in doing it with another's wife if she is not the wife of a Brahmin or a Guru. This is deception with shameless lies; as most authors of tracts used to be Brahmins, they wrote this way.[2] If an intelligent person challenges the presentations in such deceitful tracts with scriptural quotes, [the truth] will be known. It is clearly said in the *Kālachakra Tantra* that Brahmins have a black disposition for their wives.

There are many countries where uncles and nieces live together, where brother and sister live together, or brothers and sisters of the same father live together. That country where there is a society agreeing with one's own lineage has good customs.[3]

---

[1] The 1983 edition (24.9) reads *ba dha ra bi*; the 1967 edition (26.16) reads *bha dha ra bi*.

[2] Gedün Chöpel adds an interlinear note:

Similarly, the rite called *Kāmavrata* for the cleansing of women's sins prescribes such things as that she, having given pleasure to a Brahmin for thirteen months, still must offer umbrellas, gold, cows, and so forth.

[3] Gedün Chöpel adds an interlinear note:

In some areas of extreme northwest India, there are cases of the mother's staying together with the son when the father dies, etc. To speak frankly, even the reference to a treatise on taking one's mother as a wife is to Highest Yoga Tantras.

Those tantras were originally disseminated in Oḍiyāna, etc., and the lineages of humans in that area are of the *paṭhana* lineage. Although Dharmakīrti, Bhāvaviveka, and so forth later were assigned as great [tantric] adepts, when one examines these masters' own texts, it is evident that in addition to their not being acquainted with Mantra they especially avoided it. For example, in the autocommentary to his

Commentary on (Dignāga's) "Compendium of [Teachings on]
Valid Cognition" (tshad ma rnam 'grel, pramāṇavārttika)
[commenting on stanza 307 of the Svārthānumāna chapter:
Tokyo sde dge, vol. ce, 357a.4 (p. 179)] Dharmakīrti, when giving an example for the fact that a good being is not needed to
author scripture, says that nowadays it is seen that even female sky travelers (mkha' 'gro ma, dākiṇī), cannibal demons
(srin po), and so forth are composing tantras. In a similar
vein, in his Blaze of Reasoning (rtog ge 'bar ba, tarkajvālā)
Bhāvaviveka, after scorning the granting of the initiation of
Īshvara from the tip of the phallus, says:

Even when they hear the mere names of these,
People are very embarrassed ...

If one is familiar with Mantra, how could the secret initiation,
the knowledge-wisdom initiation, and so forth of our own
system not come to have the same fault!

Therefore, since the Vajra Vehicle had just spread at that
time to the areas held by the paṭhana lineage—Oḍiyāna,
Lambaka, etc.—[the mention of] a treatise on taking one's
mother as a wife is in reference to a tantra. I think that one
need not have qualms that the reference is to something else.

For a discussion of Indian and Chinese traditions concerning
polyandry and other unusual customs of extreme northwest India,
see David White, Myths of the Dog-Man (Chicago: University of
Chicago Press, 1991), Chapter Six. Thanks to Professor Donald
Lopez for the Dharmakīrti reference in the sDe dge Tibetan
Tripitaka—bsTan hgyur preserved at the Faculty of Letters, University of
Tokyo (Tokyo: 1977ff.)

3 Time

FEMALES

Forcibly doing it with a young girl produces severe pains and wounds her genitalia; consequently, later when giving birth she has difficulties. If it is not the time and if copulating would be dangerous for her, churn about between her thighs, and it will come out. In many areas it is customary to do so; it quickly promotes a girl's maturation.

Having covered with ointment the outside of a wound up cloth, make a fine, soft point. Every day raise passion [by tickling the labia]; then put it just into the vagina. Finally the phallus should enter. When a girl has matured, apply butter to the penis and slowly enter. If the phallus is churned about between the thighs, the vagina naturally gets better and ripens. Because other prescriptions for the training of girls are not needed in our country, I will put them aside.

If a girl initially menstruates during the third month,

it is said that although others will respect her, she will separate from her husband quickly.

Most girls who initially menstruate during the fourth month have virtuous minds. Their behavior is good, and their husbands will love them. Their religion and fortune will be wonderful.

A girl who initially menstruates in the fifth month will meet with great fortune. Her body will be beautiful; she will be courageous and learned and will find a learned husband who will love her.

A girl who initially menstruates in the sixth month will be in danger of sickness and will lose her children. However, she will be protected by love and will always perform the practice of charity.

A girl who initially menstruates in the seventh month will not be satisfied by copulation. All of her children will die at a young age. However, it is said that if she takes refuge in the Nāgas, this will be reversed.

A girl who initially menstruates in the eighth month will undergo awful suffering. It is said that she will be in danger of various physical illnesses and will die poor and unfortunate.

A girl who initially menstruates in the ninth month will respect her husband. She will have many children; some will die young. However, she will never be bereft of wealth.

A girl who initially menstruates in the tenth month will see her mother's household degenerate, but when staying together with her husband, she will attain glory, happiness, and comfort.

A girl who initially menstruates in the eleventh month will love her husband. She will honor monks and nuns who have good ethics. She will live on the path of true religion.

A girl who initially menstruates in the twelfth month will be skillful at the jobs of the household. Her intelligence will be clear, and she will know the treatises [i.e.,

arts of passion]. Her husband will love her, and all will
respect her.

A girl who initially menstruates in the first month will
be extremely rich. She will be wonderfully playful in all
activities. She will protect monks and nuns as well as
poor relatives.

A girl who initially menstruates in the second month
will be very happy, comfortable, and wealthy. She will
practice religion; her husband will love her, and she will
have many boys who will be conquerors over the earth.
Because Arjuna was born in this month, it is renowned
as the best from all the cycle of twelve.

The above was a rendition of the effects of the initial
menstruation for young ladies at certain times.[1]

COUPLES

A male at the age of sixteen is pubescent and at age
twenty-four is complete. A female at the age of thirteen
is pubescent and at the age of sixteen is complete.
Therefore, a male of twenty-four years and a woman of
sixteen or eighteen are at a time suitable for sex. They
may keep a home from that age. If one waits for a long
time beyond those years, it is said various illnesses will
arise. If at a young age men do it with women, they will
lose their power and will age quickly. However, if
women meet with men at a young age, it is said they
thereby forestall aging. This is not something that I
made up; I am explaining what has been proven by the
experience of old men and women.

The suffering of not getting one's desire is a burning
of the bones night and day; though for a young man

---

[1] Gedün Chöpel adds an interlinear note:

In both south India and in Shri Lanka, it is seen that, when a
young woman has her first menstruation, there is a custom
of calling Brahmins and making sacrificial offerings as well as
giving a big feast for relatives in one's home.

this suffering is great, his elders always treat it as unimportant. Even more, girls who are protected and bound by their parents have this suffering beyond measure. Therefore, when they arrive at a suitable age, male and female definitely need a way to live together.

The passion of a young woman for a man does not even compare with the thirsty's yearning for water. A passionate man's contemplation of a woman does not even compare with the hungry's desire for food. Prevention by strict parents does not even compare with being put into a dark hole. Being constrained by strict rules does not even compare with being put in stocks.

If one's expertise in renunciation is not complete, [one's passion is like] a great river which, though stopped by a dam, just breaks loose. Still, if renunciation is like a levying of taxes under an unwanted regulation, it is like trying to pull great stones uphill.

Association with a mate—brought to one by the power of previous actions (*karma*)—with love like that for one's own dear life and with abandonment of intrigues and adultery is the best of ethics. When the faculties have dulled and the mind has become peaceful, if men and women who have become gray-haired make effort at the path of religion in a place of solitude, that is the excellent behavior of earlier times. Therefore, as long as one has the wild horse of the senses and has the power of entering to the place of passion, though one partakes of the pleasures of passion, how could an intelligent being find fault!

> Living by one's own labor in accordance with
>   good teaching,
> Always doing it only with one's own wife, con-
>   trolling the senses,

And having a good time with friends who hap-
pen to arrive,
An excellent being has liberation in the home.[1]

---

[1] Gedün Chöpel adds an interlinear note:
This last stanza is from the *canakaśāstra*.

According to Professor David White, the text mentioned may be a
reference to Kauṭilya's *Arthaśāstra*, which was written for the edifi-
cation of King Canakya.

4 *Essence*

The essence of the human body is blood, and the essence of blood is seminal fluid. Ease of body, clearness of mind, and so forth mostly depend on this essence. If harm comes to the causes of this essential fluid from various bad diseases in the body and from sex with prostitutes and so forth, it is certain the family lineage of that boy will cease. Parents of such type will not produce children, and even if they do, the child will only die quickly; even if the child does not die, he or she will have physical problems. Because of this, careful behavior concerning these matters is a necessity.

It is clear that if things having shape are stirred and rubbed together, their essence will come out. For example, if two clouds mix, a stream of rain falls down, and if two sticks are rubbed together, a tongue of flame appears. Similarly, the essence of milk is butter, but at first it stays mixed in the milk. However, if it is poured into a vessel and churned, warmth arises in the milk in stages, and its essence comes out separately. Similarly, the essence of blood is seminal fluid, but at first it is dissolved in blood. However, if it is churned by the action of male and female, the power of passion raises warmth in the blood, and the seminal fluid, like butter, comes out.

Seven drops of the essence of food produce one drop of blood in the body of a human. From a cupful of blood only one tiny drop of seminal fluid is produced.

Because a woman menstruates, her physical power is less, her flesh is soft and loose, her skin is thin, her feeling is extremely sharp, and when old, she has many wrinkles. However, there are no differences in the bodies of male and female by way of external shape. Among whatever a male has, there is nothing a female does not have; even the penis and gonads are inside the female genitalia. The skin of the male collected at the root of his organ are the labia on the sides of the vagina. Underneath the labia is a small bit of flesh, about the size of a finger [the clitoris]; when passion is produced, it rises and becomes hard. It is the equivalent of the male member, and if it is tickled with a finger, passion is quickly produced in women. At the time of copulation the clitoris is so, and moreover it is said that the itch of passion is greater.

The two parts of the skin of the scrotum divided into two halves are at the sides of the vagina. Likewise, there is a womb in the male's stomach; it is the cause of the swelling of a boy's breasts.[1] In the middle of the phallus manifests a slit; that is the line of the closing of the female organ.

It is said that the women of Loṭiyaṇa in the Sindhu [Indus valley] in Greater Persia[2] are very passionate; that is well known throughout the world. They have a

---

[1] Gedün Chöpel adds an interlinear note:

Even a young male's breasts begin to swell and then diminish.

[2] *ta zig.* Most likely Pakistan.

very large clitoris; at times it even emerges outside the labia. Some can even do the deed with another woman; it is almost the size of the male member. For some, it usually is clearly outside the female genitals.

In general a girl of the West is beautiful, splendorous, and more courageous than others. Her behavior is coarse, and her face is like a man's. There is even hair around her mouth. Fearless and terrifying, she can be tamed only by passion. Able to suck the phallus at the time of play, the girl of the West is known to drink the seminal fluid. She does it even with dogs, bulls, and any other animals and with father and son, etc. She goes without hesitation with whoever can give the enjoyment of sex.

Some of the type who have a large clitoris have both sex signs or change back and forth from one to the other. There are a great many women who, from a little change in physique, have become males. Similarly, it is well known that some men whose penis retracts greatly inside have become women.

Whoever's wife has powerful passion, his family lineage will definitely all be boys. Therefore, those who wish to have boys should choose and take a passionate woman.

As an example, the Sho-mang[1] plant, which is soft and shriveled, when it is soaked by water becomes hard and swells up. Just so, when drops of blood collect together, the male and female organs erect and swell. When bliss is generated in the private parts, the mind's attention goes to that spot; by that cause, the vital winds [i.e., energies] and the blood gather, filling the middle of the male member whereupon the phallus erects.

The passion of a man is light and easy to rouse; the passion of a woman is deep and hard to rouse.

---

[1] Identified by Sarat Chandra Das, *A Tibetan-English Dictionary* (Calcutta, 1902), 1245, as a medicinal plant that clears away scars.

Therefore, if one needs purposely to raise the passion of a woman by various methods of passion, it is said that the labia and the inner nerves, the skin of the right and left sides of the mouth of the vagina, the mouth of the womb, and the points of the breasts rise and swell when passion is generated. For men the whole phallus, the pubic region, and hairy places have the feeling of bliss when passion is generated. An essential nerve is in the front of the phallus.

Still, the bliss of women is greatly spread out and unidentifiable. They have bliss everywhere beneath the navel, the top of the thighs, the inside of the vagina, the door of the womb, the anus, and the area around the buttocks. In short, all the inside and outside of the lower parts of a woman's body are pervaded by bliss, and as she can feel such bliss, it is said that the entire body of a woman is the feminine organ.

All the systems of explanation on whether women have a seminal emission disagree.[1] In the *Sūtra of Teaching to Nanda on Entry to the Womb*[2] and in the tantras of the New Translation Schools it is said that women have a seminal fluid. The followers of the master Bābhravya[3] explain that from the time of the begin-ning of the deed of copulation through to the end women have a seminal emission. Therefore, it is said that if one calculates the pleasure of passion, the female has a hundred-fold more than the male. However, oth-ers say that the feminine secretion during passion is be-ing mistaken for a seminal fluid.

Wherever the power of the mind gathers, the nerves of that sense organ are drawn together whereby inner fluids are squeezed and are emitted. When a delicious

---

[1] See the *Kāma Sūtra*, II.1.18-64.

[2] *tshe dang ldan pa dga' bo mngal du 'jug pa bstan pa, āyuṣmannanda-garbhāvakrāntinirdeśa*; P760.13, vol. 23.

[3] *Kāma Sūtra*, II.1.32.

food is contemplated, saliva flows. When embarrassed, sweat flows from the body. When passion is produced, the feminine fluid boils. When happy and sad, tears come from the eyes. Therefore, when beginning to generate passion or sorrow, etc., in the mind, if the feelings are stopped, there is no fault of hindrance, and it is very good. However, when very strong and powerful feelings are produced, if they are stopped with strictness, the force will go to the vital airs at the heart and so forth. If it is looked at from the outside, this is the reason why all those who stay off alone have too much vital air of the heart.

Even if women have a seminal fluid, aside from descending by degrees like melting ice, it does not resemble the way of us men, the sudden instantaneous emission of a great quantity. Therefore, women are not satisfied immediately after its emission and do not experience a reversal of desire as men do. Also, although after it has been emitted, one continues churning about, a woman does not find it unbearable, as men do. One woman says that as the feminine fluid gradually secretes, the vagina becomes moist, and sensitivity and bliss increase. In that case it may be that Bābhravya[1] is right [about the greater intensity of women's experience of sexual pleasure].

The master Kumāraputra[2] says that male and female do not differ with respect to the emission of seminal fluid. However, most learned persons nowadays and also women who have studied many books say that the female has no seminal fluid. Because I like conversation about the lower parts, I asked many women friends, but aside from shaking a fist at me with shame and

---

[1] The 1967 edition (43.1) reads *bha ra dha*; the 1983 edition (35.17) reads *ba dha ra*.

[2] *gzhon nu'i bu*. The Sanskrit is conjectured from the Tibetan but is tentative at best.

laughter, I could not find even one who would give an honest answer. Though the goddesses Sarasvatī and Tārā would speak honestly, they definitely do not have any.[1] When I looked myself, women do not have a seminal fluid, but there is some secretion. Whether this is a fluid or an air, if an old experienced man investigates, he will know.

On every occasion of copulation women have the final bliss. When a couple copulates several times, the first time the seminal fluid of the male is emitted quickly, and the male has more powerful passion. However, women are the opposite; it is said that the first time their passion is of little force, and the later times it increases. Therefore, men who do not emit their seminal fluid for a long time and whose phallic power does not diminish quickly give the female the glories of passion. This is what groups of women say inside the home.

It is said that the way the bliss of a woman is consummated is similar to how satisfaction is produced when itching arises in the body and a finger scratches the spot. However, it is widely known that during copulation a woman has bliss even more than seven times greater than a man. When the seminal fluid has come out, the man's bliss is finished; when the itch of passion is cleared away, the woman's bliss is finished. Therefore, if the passionate deed is done many times, it is very consuming for the body of the man, but it does not similarly harm the body of the woman. Because the vagina and the labia are uncovered[2] naked flesh, the pleasure and pain of women are extremely great, like touching the mouth of a wound.

Thus, although the way the pleasures of passion are produced in the male and female differ greatly, from

---

[1] Being beyond the world, they do not have usual physical bodies.

[2] Following the 1983 edition (37.7) which reads *g.yogs ma med pa'i* for *g.yo ba med pa yi* in the 1967 edition (44.20).

one's own individual experience, one cannot say to another, "This is it."

5 Women of Various Places

The women of the region of Ārya Rājya[1] like interesting pictures; embracing and kissing, they are thoroughly skilled in the movement of a swing.[2]

The women of Sindhu [the Indus valley][3] suck the male member, whereby they experience greater pleasure.[4]

The women of Lāṭa [Gujarat] whistle[5] and groan; they

---

[1] Since this is not in the *Kāma Sūtra*, the Sanskrit is conjectured from the Tibetan *'phags rgyal yul* (1983 edition, 37.11).

[2] The text (1983 edition, 37.13) reads *do li*, whereas the usual rendering of "swing" is *'do li*.

[3] The place identifications are taken from Bandhu, 85-87 and 295-296.

[4] This sentence is drawn from *Kāma Sūtra*, II.5.25.

[5] The Tibetan word *sid* or *sid sgra* means to whistle; Gedün Chöpel uses *sid sgra sgrogs pa* to translate the Sanskrit *sītkāra*, which means erotic sounds in general. Monier-Williams (1077) defines *śīt* or *sīt* as the sound made by drawing in the breath to express any sudden thrill of sexual pleasure. Here it seems to be an in-breath whistle.

are the type of wild burning passion.[1] At the time of copulation a great "oo" comes out; it is said that it can be heard three fences away.

The women of Gandhārva[2] are white and of medium size. Their huge hips enclose the vagina. They drink beer of good color and fragrant odor and always pass the time with conversation about sex.

From the vagina of the women of Draviḍa a white fluid is secreted before copulation.

The women of Gauḍa [West Bengal] and Kāmarūpa [Assam, Manipur] are very loose; it is said that if a man only touches a hand, they follow and give him pleasure.

The women of Gujarāt have a roving eye and a thin, weak body. Their breasts are large, and their hair is like flowers; they are filled with passion inside and outside.

In the city of Yāmā[3] itching arises in the woman's organ from time to time; hence she urges men to copulate with her and uses a wooden dildo. It is well known that in places where there are only women the deed is always done this way.

The women of Koṅkana [Southern Karnataka] in the south, without knowing their own faults, blame others; they bite and pinch, etc., but if a man does so, they deride and accuse him.

The women of Aṅgabhaṅgala[4] and Kaliṅga [Southern Bengal] are queens of passion; they bite and pinch and like to be pressed hard. They are the type that are not satisfied no matter how often it is done. They continually use a male member made from leather.

Except for the city of Pāṭaliputra[5] [Patna], the girls of

---

[1] This sentence is drawn from *Kāma Sūtra*, II.5.26.

[2] Since this is not in the *Kāma Sūtra*, the Sanskrit is conjectured from the Tibetan *dri za* (1983 edition, 37.18).

[3] Conjectured from the Tibetan *'thab bral* (1983 edition, 38.9).

[4] Aṅgavaṅga is Bengal.

[5] *skya nar bu.*

the cities of the central region on the banks of the Gangā and Yamunā Rivers produce noble lineages. They are peaceful, and as it is difficult for them even to kiss at the time of copulation, they find it unsuitable to bite or pinch at all.[1] The women of the western region Mahārāshtra are the passionate type burning like fire. When copulating, they cry and bite; they use all of the sixty-four arts.[2] They like various forms of sex, using unusual deeds to generate special satisfaction. They suck the male member with their mouths and make wounds on his body with their teeth.

Though the women of the city of Pāṭaliputra [Patna] are the burning passion type, they are not straightforward, feigning disinterest. They always do it in secret.

The women of the region of the Panjab, Mālava,[3] south of Bāhanika, are pleased with embracing and kissing; it is said that at the time of copulation they need it a long time.

A woman of Bāhlika[4] [Multan District] is rapacious. She embraces one, and another works her; she kisses another and plays with another; it is said she plays with even five men together. Similarly, all the parts of a man's body are played with by many women.

In Vidarbha [Barar] relatives do not protect their women. It is done with all, suitable and unsuitable.

The women of the city of Sāketa[5] and of Saurasana are all accustomed to oral sex.[6] Just so, it is seen that the

---

[1] This paragraph is mostly drawn from *Kāma Sūtra*, II.5.21.

[2] These two sentences are drawn from *Kāma Sūtra*, II.5.29.

[3] The Tibetan (1983 edition) reads *ma la ya*, but the description mostly fits that of *Kāma Sūtra*, II.5.24.

[4] For a discussion of Bāhlika women, see David White, *Myths of the Dog-Man*, 120-121.

[5] *gnas bcas.*

[6] In an interlinear note Gedün Chöpel identifies this in Sanskrit as

women on the banks of the Chandrabhaga[1] [Chenab] River mostly desire the deeds of the mouth.

When the women of Arhara copulate, the mouth of the vagina always closes; they do it in the manner of the mare.

In the area of Chaula there is wild sex; they do crazy customs of beating, striking, and biting. It is well known that a girl called Chitrasenā,[2] wounded in all her body, died.

The women in the kingdom of Aparātaka [northern Koṅkaṇa] in north India are unstable, and their love affairs are of little duration.

The women of Kembajali are extremely skillful in the opening and closing of the vagina; it is said that even if the male member is small and does not rise, they can give the full pleasure of copulation. In general the lineages of men in that area are seen to have small organs and diminutive physical strength.

The women of Laṅka are bluish of color and their waists are supple; though their vaginas are loose, they are skilled at the arts of motion. With their legs embracing the neck of the man, they experience the pleasures of copulation.

The girls of Kunlanta are powerful and fat and have hard breasts and vagina.

The women of Suvarṇa[3] have beautiful faces; they stay sleepily without moving, like a corpse. Similarly, the women of southeastern areas are known for their extremely slight enjoyment of sex.

The women of Kapila and Uḍiyāna are of a demonic type. Their vaginas are like burning fire, with their

---

mukhamaithuna (oral union). The 1983 edition (40.3) and the 1967 edition (48.18) read *mu kha ma thun*.

[1] *zla cha*.

[2] *ri mo'i sde*. See *Kāma Sūtra*, II.7.27.

[3] Conjectured from the Tibetan *gser yul* (1983 edition, 41.1).

secretion always boiling. As they have unbearable passion, they use crazy techniques.

In the land of Kuru[1] and the region of Kanyakubja as well as in the Moslem kingdom of Kusha in the western quarter where the Seven Falls River runs it is said there are many amazingly beautiful girls.

Women who drink the water of the snow of the Himalayas which has fallen from the rocks of mountaintops and which bears the essence of the king lizard[2] have an essence of fire.

The above was mostly set forth in the *Kāma Sūtra*;[3] the areas mentioned are only in India. Also, because they are ancient customs, it is not certain that they exist nowadays. The master Suvarṇanābha[4] explains that because lineages of humans gathered in cities, the individual customs of the various women were learned by all, and hence they continually changed. Nevertheless, it is definitely true that the natures of humans in each area are mostly similar.

These natures of women should be explained through associating them also with the country of Tibet, but because I have had acquaintance with none other than women of Kam[5] and Dzang,[6] I do not have detailed understanding. The women of Kam have soft flesh and are very affectionate. The women of Dzang are skilled in technique; they are good at moving about beneath a man.

---

[1] *sgra ngan.*

[2] Lizard flesh is renowned as an aphrodisiac.

[3] Not even a quarter of the above material is drawn from the *Kāma Sūtra* itself; little also could be attributed to Kokkoka's *Ratirahasya*.

[4] The text (1983 edition, 41.15) reads *su be ra.* See *Kāma Sūtra*, II.5.34, for part of this idea. Suvarṇanābha was the expositor of the second section of Bābhravya's work, on sexual union.

[5] *khams* the southeastern province of Tibet.

[6] *gtsang*; the western province of Tibet.

This little outline of the women of Tibet was written for the sake of calling other passionate persons to the task. Here the methods of lying, moving, and so forth of the women of Am-do, Kam, Central Tibet, Ḍzang, and Ṅga-ri[1] could be added by a knowledgeable old man who has experienced the world.

This was the section describing the behavior of women of individual areas.

---

[1] *mnga' ris.*

6 Embracing

If, like fearful thieves eating a meal, a couple just rubs together quietly and gently on a dark bed and the seminal fluid is emitted, it is not a complete party of passion. Therefore, passionate men and women should know the sixty-four arts of passion that bring out the tastes of bliss, various like the tastes of molasses, milk, and honey. Whatever woman knows well the forms of passion crazing a man's mind and can infatuate him at the time of pleasure is called the best of women.

There are sixty-four arts of passion, dividing each of the eight—embracing, kissing, pinching and scratching, biting, pressing, making erotic noises, ways of copulation, and the activities of the man [done by the woman]—into eight.[1] Sucking, slapping, and caressing with the tongue, there are innumerable uncertain deeds,

---

[1] Gedün Chöpel reverses the order of the last two in the exposition that follows. In the *Kāma Sūtra* (II.2.5) Bābhravya's list of eight includes oral sex (which Gedün Chöpel is about to list as additional) and does not give a section for "ways of copulation" separate from "pressing".

such as *mukhamaithuna*[1] (oral sex), for extremely passionate males and females.

The Eight Embraces

(1) Seeking a pretext for conversation, one touches the naked shoulders of a new person—such as in a narrow passageway or when picking up and putting down articles. This is called **touching,** *spṛṣṭaka*.[2]

(2) In a solitary place, she places her wrists on the back of her man's neck and touches him with the points of the breasts. This is called **piercing,** *viddhaka*.

(3) Using wild arts with thoughtless passion, he squeezes the woman against a wall and bites her cheek and shoulder. This is called **pressing,** *pīḍitaka*.[3]

(4) The two hands of the female embrace the man's neck; as the two mutually touch stomachs, the man grasps the woman and raises her up. This is called **twining creeper,**[4] *latāsveṣṭha*.

(5) The woman puts one foot on the waist of the male and with the other presses the toes of his foot; her hands bend his head to her, and they kiss. This is called **tree-climbing**.

(6) They mutually bind thighs with thighs; she points her breasts at the male's chest and shakes the upper part of the body with a gazing stare. This is called **wind shaking the palmyra tree**.

(7) With passion fully burning like a fire they stand or lie down; after embracing, the woman points her lower body at that [of the man], and they join together. This is

---

[1] The 1983 edition (43.5) misreads *mu kha me mun*; the 1967 edition (52.18) misreads *mu kha le bdun*. *Mukhamaithuna* literally means "mouth-union".

[2] Gedün Chöpel occasionally gives Sanskrit names for the acts of love. The Sanskrit terms have the same meaning as the English terms immediately preceding them.

[3] Both texts (1983, 43.14; 1967, 53.12) misread *pīṭitaka*.

[4] The 1983 edition (43.16) misreads *'khril*.

called **form of a fluttering flag.**[1]

(8) Both are swallowed in the obscurity of passion, and putting breast to breast and genitals to genitals, embrace naked in a bed. This is called **mixture of water and milk.**

> Aroused with these forms, women let down
> Their hair, kiss, and caress the phallus—
> Becoming wish-granting cows fulfilling all
>   thoughts
> Without feigning and embarrassment.

Those are the forms of embrace.

---

[1] It is likely that the woman shakes and twists her hips, aiming them at the male, and thus this embrace is said to be like a fluttering flag.

7 Kissing

(1) When a man and a woman who were formerly acquainted meet again, at first with happy face they both touch cheeks and kiss. This is called **mutual acknowledgment,** *pratibodha*.

(2) To a girl whose face is timid pinch her neck and kiss her ear as well as the crown of her head. This form is called **initial kissing**.

(3) A young girl who has drunk with oneself the beer of passion and the honey of embarrassment gives a kiss vibrating with the opening and closing of her lips. This is called **throbbing,** *sphuritaka*.

(4) A woman through a change of aspect rubs the man's body with lips and tongue. As this is a sign of having engendered pleasure, it is called a **sign,** *nimitaka*.

(5) Averting the eye due to the pangs of passion[1] and putting the cheek to the nose,[2] kiss, gently rubbing the

---

[1] The 1983 edition (45.5) reads *'dod pa'i dmod pa babs pas*; the 1967 edition (55.15) reads *'dod pa'i gnod pa babs pa'i*.

[2] The 1983 edition (45.5) reads *sna*; the 1967 edition (55.15) reads *rna*

inside of the mouth with the tip of the tongue. This is called **waterwheel**, *ghaṭika*.

(6) The male kisses all places on the female. Immediately after, the female answers his kisses at those same places. This is called **after-kiss**, *uttara*.

(7) The mouth of the male sucks[1] and kisses the stomach of the woman lying down, and his cheek rubs the hollows of her waist. This is called **jewel-case**, *piṭaka*.

(8) Intoxicated with passion and unsatisfied, the woman kisses the extended phallus. The joyous force comes out, and with intoxication she drinks. Those are the eight kisses of great enjoyment.

Ears, throat, cheeks, armpits, lips, thighs, stomach, breasts, and vagina—these focal spots are the nine places of kissing. Determine the suitable and the unsuitable according to your own thought. In particular, the area from beneath the breasts to the knees is tamed by only the touch of sex.

In short, the places of the body that are usually not touched by others have great sensitivity. It is said that the areas from which heat and moisture arise and all the hollows of flesh that produce hair are doors of passion.

Again and again gaze at all nine places. Bite the nine places. Rub and suck the nine places. Determine the suitable and the unsuitable according to your own thought.

Moreover, because the physical essence moves about the places of the body day by day, it is said that if those places are kissed and so forth at certain times, passion increases greatly. From dawn until twelve midnight on the sixteenth day [of the lunar month] the essence stays at the top of the head. Similarly, on the seventeenth it is at the ears, and on the eighteenth, at the nose. Then

---

(ear).

[1] In the 1967 edition (55.4) read *gzhib* for *gzhin* in accordance with The 1983 edition (45.10).

from the nineteenth until the end of the month day by day it moves to the mouth, cheeks, shoulders, chest, stomach, navel, waist, pubic region, thighs, knees, calves, and upper part of the feet. Again, on the first of the month it is at the calves, and the second, the knees; on the third likewise it is at the thighs. Similarly apply the remaining body-parts to the days until the fifteenth, when it pervades the whole body.

At first kiss the shoulders, then the armpits,
And then slowly move to the stomach.
If greatly aroused and mischievous, kiss the
    thighs and vagina.
Draw the water in the canals to the lake.

Those are the activities of kissing.

8 Pinching and Scratching

Making erotic noises, laughing, clamoring, slapping each other, biting and pinching hard, and alternating top to bottom—this is called the battle of male and female in passionate sex. Intoxicated biting, grasping hard, and seeking an opportunity for copulation with rough play—these natural deeds of passion occur in the animals of the forest on up.

(1) As preparation, the face of pleasure is revealed; groans and noises are made; his arms enclose her waist, and on her breasts he pinches a little, leaving marks like grains of rice. This is called **like-scratches**, *ācchurita*.[1]

(2) Lick from the mouth of her vagina to her navel, and with the back of the thumbnail press and rub. This causes the woman to itch a great deal; it is called **long line**, *dirgarekha*.

(3) With a flush face of boiling passion, embrace her chest and breasts like a conqueror. Each rubs the back

---

[1] The 1983 edition (47.8) misreads *acchurita*; the 1967 edition (82.5) misreads *acchurata*.

of the other downwards with the fingernails. This is called **mark of a tiger**.

(4) She squeezes his phallus in the palm of her hand and presses with her thumb. With the other four fingers put together, she presses and circles the root of his organ. This is called **circle**, *maṇḍala*.

(5) With his hands he takes hold of the flesh of a thigh and a breast and strongly pinches with four fingernails and at times lifts and rubs at the shoulder blades. This is called **form of a half moon**.

(6) He squeezes with his fingers her nipples and the mouth of the place of reproduction, pinching hard with his thumbnails. Four finger marks are imprinted there. This is called **mark of a peacock's foot**.

(7) With great intoxication scratch and scratch and pinch the back and behind with four fingers. This is called **marks of a jumping rabbit**. After the one does it, the other bows and begins.

(8) On the top of the shoulder, between the shoulders, the chest, and the stomach scratch with all five fingernails, whereby deep red nail marks appear. This is called **lotus petals**.

To the thighs, behind, and breasts make very red deep nail marks. Feel with the outstretched fingers the armpits, top of the head, phallus, and vagina, and pinch without wound. It is also said that at times it is suitable to pinch with wounds the shoulders, neck, and back of the shoulders. It is said that until the wounds heal and disappear, the enjoyment of passion is not forgotten.

The purposes of pinching and scratching are to overcome the shrunkenness of the fascinating limb, to distract the mind, to relieve itching in the body, and to convey inner strong inner passion. It is said that later when parting, if man and woman pinch hard with fingernails on the chest and top of the head, it helps to remember and not forget. It is claimed that this is the reason for the orange mark on the top of the woman's head.

When meeting, pinch the neck and shoulders. When close to entering the vagina, pinch the breasts. When copulating, pinch the back and waist. When emitting, rub the spinal column. As long as he has no embarrassment of the naked woman, as long as he chokes at the throat and the water of desire falls, as long as the seminal fluid approaches coming out, until then bite and pinch. When the man is approaching emission, the woman's pinching strongly the upper part of his ears will cause the seminal fluid to come out quickly. Also, sometimes it helps to pinch the armpits.

Having become accustomed to the activities of pinching, even the deed will not produce satisfaction without it. In many areas passionate women strongly desire the touch of fingernails, and doing the deed without biting and pinching is considered to be like doing it without kissing.

9 Biting

After they first meet, when passion increases or they approach the time of sex, he should press, push, slap with the palm, pull her hair, and bite.

(1) Along with agitating the body and making sounds, he kisses the nape of her neck. Then he gently squeezes her lower lip between his teeth. This is called **dots,** *guḍaka.*

(2) Kissing intensely and touching teeth to teeth, strongly bind the lip with the teeth; the mark of it later is a swelling. This is called **swelling,** *ucchunaka.*

(3) Face approaches face, and words of passion are spoken. Two fine tooth marks are set between the lower lip and the chin. This is known as **drops of ambrosia.**

(4) Mark the cheeks and shoulders with the imprint of biting, and a red series of dots will appear. This is called **coral jewels.**

(5) Press the naked woman on a pillow, and gaze at all her body, high and low. Then bite all the fleshy parts.

This is called **series of drops**, *bhindumāla*.[1]

(6) With intoxication and longing, again and again set the teeth to the upper part of the breasts and the cheeks of the backside, making marks one above the other. This is called **pieces of clouds**.

(7) Mouth joins mouth, and the tongue and lips are sucked hard and drawn between the teeth, then pulled a little. This is called **anthers of a flower**, *puṣpakeśa*.

(8) In that way, after strong passion has manifestly arisen, join the mouth to the cheeks, armpits, and places beneath the navel; press with the lower teeth and rub upwards. This is called **poplar root**.

> Changing all forms—beautiful, smiling, and ap-
> propriate—
> Like the creations of a magician, the Great
> Fearful Woman
> With the flush face of laughter, blazing
> With the cast of blood, is called a pouch of pas-
> sion.[2]

Those are the forms of biting.

---

[1] The 1983 text (50.10) reads *bhindumala*.

[2] Following the 1983 edition (51.3) which reads *chags pa'i rkyal bar brjod*; the 1967 edition (63.20) reads *chags pa'i rgyal bar mdzod*.

10 Ways of Pleasure

Immediately upon seeing the marks of fingernails on the breasts of a young woman and seeing the marks of a woman's teeth on the body of a man, even a queen's thought suddenly wavers, and her composure fades. It is claimed[1] that a female messenger whose lips have the blood of wounds and whose body is covered with deep marks of fingernails of a young man's fierce passion deceives the mistress. It is said that even through giving flowers, fruits, molasses, articles, and so forth despoiled with marks of teeth and fingernails, passion attracts and controls the mind.

Draw the form of the deed of copulation of wild animals on the leaves of the Nandakaras tree and show it to her stealthily in a solitary place. It is said a princess is thereby controlled.

The putting of marks like those of biting beneath the lower lips of women is still seen in some parts of India.

---

[1] Through a grammatically unsuitable ending (*so lo*) Gedün Chöpel indicates his disagreement with this assertion.

It is claimed[1] that the amount of passion produced [thereby in the man] is an adornment of the woman. This passion which comes to all men and women without striving and by their very nature is covered with a little embarrassment; if one makes a little effort at it, its nature will nakedly show itself. Look at a drawing of a sleeping nude; look at horses and cattle copulating; write out and read treatises on passion; tell various stories of passion.

Even though youth has passed, as long as passion has not subsided, the channels and juices will stay warm whereby even physical prowess, inside and out, will not diminish.

The innate bliss is non-artificial and self-arisen, but all the world wears a mask of pretension. Therefore, at the time of pleasure male and female should abandon all customs and feigning.

Who can distinguish the clean and the dirty in the upper and lower parts of the body? By what can the upper and lower parts of the body be assigned as good or bad? That the upper part is satisfactory and the lower part is hidden is unremarkable good behavior.

> The rivers of an area augment its beauty;[2]
> The thorns of prejudice are only roots of illness.
> Without meditation one can cease prejudices,
> And an ordinary person will have the bliss of sex.

> bāhumūlakucadvandvayo
> nisparśanadarśanat
> kasya na skhalati citta retaḥ
> skanna ca no bhavet[3]

---

[1] Through a grammatically unsuitable ending (*yin lo*) Gedün Chöpel indicates his disagreement with this assertion.

[2] Translation doubtful. The 1983 edition (52.13) reads *yul gyi rba klung sdug gi bsnon pa ste*; the 1967 edition (66.3) reads *yul gyi rba klung sdug gi snon ma ste.*

[3] The next stanza is a Tibetan translation of these four lines of

There is no one whose firmness of mind does not
    diminish
And whose seminal fluid does not drip
From looking at and caressing the shoulders,
Breasts, and genitals of a woman.

susnigdharomarahitaṃ
pakkāśatthadalākṛti
darśayiṣyami tat sthānaṃ
kāmageho sugandhica[1]

I will teach in the presence
Of the fragrant home of passion,
Resembling the shape of a mature leaf of the
    bodhi tree,
Devoid of hair where the soft wet fluid boils.[2]

Just as much as a man becomes passionate, so much a
skillful woman touches, raises, and shows her breasts

Buddhist hybrid Sanskrit (1983 edition, 52.15). Professor Karen Lang
reconstructs the standard Sanskrit as:
bāhumūlakucadvandvayo[r] nisparśanadarśanāt/
kasya na skhalati citta[ṃ] retaḥskanna[ś] ca no bhavet//
She renders this in English as:
From looking at and caressing [her] shoulders and breasts,
Whose mind does not waver and whose seminal fluid would
    not drip?

[1] The next stanza is a Tibetan translation of these four lines of
Buddhist hybrid Sanskrit (1983 edition, 52.19). Professor Karen Lang
reconstructs the standard Sanskrit as:
susnigdharomarahitaṃ pakvāśvatthadalākṛti[ṃ]/
darśayiṣyāmi tat sthānaṃ kāmageh[aṃ] sugandhi[kaṃ]//
She renders this in English as:
I will show that place, a fragrant abode of sensual pleasure,
As having the shape of a mature leaf of the bodhi-tree, very
    smooth and without bristles.

[2] Gedün Chöpel follows this material with an interlinear note:
These two stanzas were taken from the *History of
Padmasambhava* (*padma'i sngon rabs*).

and inebriates him even more with words of passion. She groans and kisses again and again and, aiming her chest and lower parts, embraces. With the form of complete intoxication and with no clothes at all she makes her body naked. Then forsaking all attitudes of embarrassment, with the sexy face of burning passion, she looks at the male's hard phallus. She rocks, rubs, and strokes it with her hand, inebriating him.

Alas, the king of pleasure gives the path of life
To the women of the world.
Take the power of a life wishing for the hard and
    stable
To this whirlpool of passion with waves of love.

In the box filled with the flesh of the lower part
Of the body of this young naked mature woman,
Born to show and give the pleasure of pleasures,
Resides the essence of all the pleasure of plea-
    sures.

Put the flower of feigning behind the ear.
Give away the plant of doubt as the food of
    birds.
The female fish of embarrassment is carried
    away by a black female crow.
Whatever one is not, one is at this time.

Seeing the arrow of passion not drawn on the
    bow of flowers,
The jewel[1] filled with the milk of ambrosia,
And that with the oily red color of coral,
Even the daughters of the gods will fall to the
    ground.

Merely touching with the tip of the jewel is the
    taste.
Entering is the delicious molasses itself.

---

[1] Head of the phallus.

Rubbing and pressing are the sweet honey.
Give to me the various delicious sweet tastes.

It is raised up like the back of a turtle and has a mouth-door closed in by flesh—the lotus-entrance, burning with the warmth of passion and intoxicating. See this smiling thing with the brilliance of the fluid of passion. It is not a flower with a thousand petals nor a hundred; it is a mound endowed with the sweetness of the fluid of passion. The refined essence of the juices of the meeting of the play of the white and red [fluids of male and female], the taste of self-arisen honey is in it.

Wear shiny black braids on the sides of the neck. Tie a finger-ring[1] on the waist, and wear an anklet as an ear ring. The man should equal the behavior of his woman-friend.

Wavering soft breasts, beautiful chest, a youthful body with robust round limbs and with lower parts having the weight of solid flesh, the body of a woman is a mound of veritable honey.

Having clearly seen the intoxicating lotus of ambrosia between her plump thighs, like a spring bull penetrate a girl, a pool of desire.[2] Press with the chest a passionate girl with curvaceous waist and movement swift like a fish. By swimming in the lake of passion even the particles of the body become just blissful and joyous.

The above expressed the ways of pleasure.

---

[1] Specified as a *nor bu'i 'og pags* (1983 edition, 54.15).

[2] A pool, or swamp, is where a lotus blooms; the female genitalia is often compared to a lotus.

11 *Playing with the Organ*

Immediately after meeting, entering with ardent desire and immediately after entering, emitting the seminal fluid, this is the way a dog gulps down lungs. Through it not even a little pleasure is found.

Desiring the fire of passion burning strong, enter to the place of the sacrament of passion. This bed where the friction base of a beautiful woman is laid is just set up for pleasure.

Place the right foot on the man's shoulder, showing clearly the breasts and vagina. With a damp palm strike the middle of your own place of reproduction. Then like the mystical dagger of the occultist, always in secret with many methods, begin any and all forms of very passionate play on the flower that is the organ of manifest pleasure.

Embracing firmly the man's neck with your left arm, kiss again and again. Stretching the right hand, take hold of the waist of the phallus and milk it like the teat of a cow.

Likewise, wrap it between the two palms; pull a little, turn it right and left. Take hold of the root, and then shaking each other, strike the thighs, lips, and teeth.

Between the two stomachs squeeze and rub the man's erect phallus. Sometimes bind it between the thighs, and rub it in the mouth-door of the vagina.

Putting the phallus between the fingers, gaze at it with extremely passionate eyes. Take a handful of the scrotum, and rub again and again the main nerves of the pubic region.

While stroking his buttocks with your hands, touch and rub with the point of the phallus the hollows of your stomach, throat, bosom, and so forth—the places where itching and passion rise. With the tips of the breasts and the tips of the fingers, touch the hole from which the seed emerges. If especially intoxicated and stirred with passion, rub that hole with the tongue and suck.

With your fingers raise itching in the area of the root [of the organ], and with your hand put the smooth jewel in. Again and again, put it in the mouth-door of the vagina. Put it half way in and take it out.

Because it gives an excellent lineage and the glories of pleasure and because it is the essence of life and has the nature of one's innate deity, it is said that even slight prohibition of intoxicating deeds at the time of pleasure is a sinful doctrine.

If the deed of copulation is done when the woman generates a force of passion greater than the man, the power of pleasure is maintained, and there is no doubt of conception and birth of a boy.

> Whatever woman enhances the self-arisen phal-
> lus
> With the petals of her mouth
> Pleases the great bliss-bestowing goddess.

She will attain glory, wealth, and the supreme of boys.

The above has indicated play with the organ.

12 Moving To and Fro and Pressing

The hearts of both vibrate with passion; they look with flush faces free from shame. She pulls the jewel of the organ [i.e., the head of the phallus] with her hand and enters it into the hole of her vagina. Entering only the tip, she takes it out again and again. She sends in half; again and again she takes it out. Finally she puts it all the way in and aims it upward for a long time.

With her legs pulled up, she pushes the man's buttocks [with her feet]. Her knees touch under his arm pits, and with her thighs and calves she binds and rubs downward.

Sometimes when the phallus comes out, the woman holds it with her hand and shakes it; again she rolls it between her first three fingers and sends it in. When it completely disappears, she gently rocks the scrotum and squeezes well the root of the phallus with two fingers; then she rotates it inside the vagina.

Having pressed two or three times, again and again rock and wipe the tip of the phallus with a soft cloth.

Through this it will become very bulbous and hard. Sometimes also wipe the door of the vagina. Keep the area around the root of the phallus moist; wipe again and again the tip and middle. Girlfriends who want to partake of powerful pleasures should learn this quintessential instruction.

Then, with lust for sex especially burning, the male is to be put below. Like a fish circling a fish, from one side of a wide bed to the other they roll and switch positions while embracing each other.

As much passion as there is, there are tears, and as much attention as there is, there is expression. If by those two the fences of embarrassment are crossed, the nature of pleasure becomes very powerful. Do the deed of passion in the ways that you like it in all its forms, and taste all the forms of pleasure described in the various commentaries. When both become intoxicated with strong passion due to being well acquainted, trusting, and without qualms, during sex do not refrain from anything; do everything without exception. Those who have secret uncommon meetings unsuitable to be seen by a third party or heard by a fifth ear become the best of bosom friends in the world.

Thus led on the path of manifest intoxication by various arts of passion, the two types of women, hard and dripping, should proceed on the path of pleasure in accordance with their wishes. Not changing in body and mind and difficult to raise her passion, this type of woman is known as hard. Quickly changing composure and generating the moisture of the feminine secretion, this type is known as dripping.

If the man is quick, the first copulation does not produce satisfaction in the woman. Thus those with power and much seminal fluid should do it two or three times. Otherwise, when the seminal fluid is about to come out, desist from movement and spread out the pleasure; again when passion rises, do it. Still, it is said that whatever is done, two times are needed.

Immediately after the seminal fluid has been emitted, the male member should not be taken out; keep it deep in the vagina. Let her shake and move as she wants in order to consummate her pleasure. If her pleasure still is not complete, the man should enter two fingers in her vagina and stir.

In general, before copulation it is essential that with two fingers he rubs and caresses the hole of the vagina.

In addition, at the beginning rub again and again the inside of the reproductive organ with a male member made of wood, and when the woman becomes aroused, do the deed.

In the southern regions[1] this custom is still performed. When the husband goes away, the women do it to themselves. It is said that the rich will have one made even of gold, silver, brass, or the like. In India most women only know their own husbands, and as sex that fulfills expectations is rare, this custom of secrecy is very prevalent. Similarly, harems protected by eunuchs[2] always resort to this. Stories of this have risen in our country, and in the *Kāma Sūtra* it is given as advice.[3]

By the husband's being too fast, it is said a woman will not experience sexual pleasure even once in three years. It would be good for a man who does not know thus the inner experience of his wife and life-long friend to be a hermit!

In short, the essence of all these treatises on passion is

---

[1] *lho lam.*

[2] *nyug rum dag*: 1983 edition, 60.14. It is noteworthy that Gedün Chöpel does not use the term *ma ning* (*paṇḍaka*) which many scholars have mistakenly translated as "eunuch". For a very clear and thorough discussion of the term *paṇḍaka*, see Leonard Zwilling, "Homosexuality as Seen in Indian Buddhist Texts", in *Buddhism, Sexuality, and Gender*, edited by José Ignacio Cabezón, 203-214.

[3] See, for instance, *Kāma Sūtra* II.6.6 and VII.2.

not to actually perform the act of sex until strong feel-ings of passion are produced in the woman by various deeds. It is said that signs that the woman has become very aroused are the rising of the clitoris at the secret gate, shaking, flesh vibrating, warmth burning, genera-tion of the feminine secretion, a flush face, and unmov-ing eyes. If without the woman's being wound round completely with passion he forces himself on her against her wish and does the deed, it is the way of lower beings, a mass of sin. Though she conceives, it will only be a daughter.

However, women are bashful such that they always shy away from loud noises. Thus they find it difficult to assent to the counsel of passion. Therefore, it is always hard for them to perform the deeds of the male.

Even the mutual smiles of male and female, if it is thought about well, have the meaning of sex. Hence without choosing good or bad, taking it as one finds it should be considered a suitable time.

The good foolish man who himself binds himself with chains, not through renunciation, not through religion, not through the right way, and not through vows, uses up his life this way. Similarly, the hidden deeds of those passionate persons in disguise—making effort at pre-tension and so forth—are said to be just axes chopping away at their basic physical constituents.

The woman, lying on her back, puts her two heels side by side, and the man grasps them with his hands; then he raises them up to her lap and does the deed. This is call the **crab**, *karkaṭaka*. Sometimes, her knees moving like the ears of a elephant, she slaps them against the sides of the male. Sometimes the woman, lying on her back, stays in a cross-legged posture, with the male beneath her, doing it as before. Sometimes he ties her feet with a rope of cloth. Sometimes the woman herself holds her legs.

The woman lies down on her back with her front side

upward; she draws up her knees and opens her thighs. Both kiss, embrace, and agitate. This is an easy way; in most areas all do it. It is called **cow-herd lying supine**. The woman kneels and opens her thighs; her two arms hug the shoulders of the male. The male also kneels and with his two hands squeezes the right and left breasts of the female. Both place the upper part of the body a distance apart; this is [called] **widely opened**, *utphullaka;*[1] gaze at her breasts and vagina.

The man places a thigh between the thighs of the woman, and he likewise binds a thigh of the woman. Both stretch out their legs, and they do it. This is called **Indra's consort**, *indrāṇika.*[2]

> With the woman underneath, do it from above.
> With the woman mounting the man, do it.
> Similarly, with both lying on their sides, do it.
> Sometimes do it from the back.
>
> Sitting, do it. Standing, do it.
> Reversing head and feet and embracing, do it.
> Likewise, with a rope of cloth
> Suspend her legs in the air and do it.

From among these eight fundamental methods of copulation, in the secrecy of your home enlarge upon whatever you wish. Do not suddenly do one which without familiarity and practice could hurt nerves, bones, flesh, and so forth.

(1)[3] The woman lies down on her back. He spreads her thighs and puts a cushion under her rear raising her

---

[1] The 1983 edition (62.17) and the 1967 edition (79.14) read *utpallaka*.

[2] The 1983 edition (63.2) and the 1967 edition (79.19) misread *iṇḍanika*.

[3] Given the sometimes extensive descriptions, it is difficult to determine the eight that Gedün Chöpel intended, and thus the numbers that are added for the sake of ease in reading should be taken as tentative.

vagina. The woman puts both feet on the man's spinal column, and he does it firmly all the way to the root of the pubic region.

He grasps her with his hands and pulls her downward. He presses his toes against the wall, pressing upward. He pulls out up to the head of his phallus and pushes in, joining the roots of their pubic regions.

They put mouth to mouth and rub each other with their chests. The woman embraces the man around his behind with her arms. From time to time he rubs her breasts, and from time to time she rocks his gonads. This is the ultimate sweetness for passionate persons. It is known as **juice of molasses, *guḍaudaka*.**[1]

The man grasps her well with his hands at the hollows of her knees and raises her up. The woman clasps her hands around the man's neck and hangs her head and upper parts outward. Only her hips rest on the pubic region of the man. The woman herself does the action of a swing. Sometimes the man sits on a seat, and sometimes he sits in a cross-legged posture. If strong, it is also suitable to walk about. The device of a suspension rope is also useful. This method can be employed on many occasions.

(2) [Lying on her stomach] with her thighs together, she stretches her legs out straight with force; he mounts her from the top like a horse and does it. She presses hard with the sides of her thighs. If appropriate, put a cushion under her middle. This is called **powerful, *sārita*.** It is extremely wonderful and bestows the tastes of pleasure. All who are passionate are just enthusiastic for this.

(3) The woman, lying down, puts her two heels on the right and left sides of the male's stomach. She rubs with her heels and raises the man up. This is called

---

[1] The 1983 edition (64.2) and the 1967 edition (82.5) misread *guḍadaka*.

rocking, *preṃkha*.[1]

The woman embraces the man's waist with one leg. The other she puts on a shoulder or the crown of his head. This is called a waving head; the union is tight, bestowing the thrills of passion.

(4) With both either standing or kneeling, while doing and doing, they lean the upper body outward. Holding fingers, they just touch to the ground. This is called **pressing down**, *nipātaka*.[2]

(5) Both rise and touch sex signs. Moving in front and behind each other, they do it. Sometimes the woman leans against a wall. This is called **standing copulation**. Sometimes he leans his back against a wall, the woman gently moving her hinder parts.

(6) He places the derriere of the woman on a table and puts her two feet on his shoulders. From the front he spreads and raises her thighs and does it. Both sex signs will meet at the root; hence, this is called **nothing between**; it especially produces satisfaction in a passionate woman. Another form of this is to tie her ankles and carry them on his back. If it becomes uncomfortable, put them on the shoulder blades and back. Again, another form is for the man to grasp both legs with his hands and open them wide. That it is extremely pleasurable is known from putting it to practice.

(7) The man sits in the cross-legged posture leaning a little back; the woman sits on his lap with her two thighs spread. Her arms embrace his shoulders, on the top or sides, and she puts her two feet on the ground in back of the man. This is called **partaking pleasure**. The woman does the pulling out and entering. Done mostly with the movement of a swing, it is very pleasurable.

---

[1] The 1983 edition (64.17) misreads *pre kha ṅa*; the 1967 edition (82.7) misreads *sro kha ṅa*.

[2] The 1983 edition (65.4) misreads *ni pra ta ka*; the 1967 edition (82.7) misreads *ni sra ta ka*.

Another way is to put a high cushion under the rear of the squatting woman. The man puts his two heels at his buttocks and from the sides of his thighs spreads her two legs backwards. He enters her pubic region and meets her. In this the action of entering and coming out is done by the man. It is said that it gives superior enjoyment of bliss.

In that, with the mouth of the vagina and the root of the phallus joined tightly and without pushing and pulling, like a swing hanging from the tree of the shoulders, move the lower body to the right and left, the head of the phallus touching and touching the insides of the vagina. This is called the movement of a swing. Many women like this. Do it in accordance with the experience of the woman.

It is suitable for either the man or both to do the work of entering inside and coming outside. This is called the movement of a pestle. Also, sometimes pull out crooked from the side, pulling it out only halfway.

(8) Like a bee in the anthers of a lotus, while vibrating the lower part of her body embraced by your arms, rotate the posterior of the woman round and round.[1] This is known as **form of a wheel** and **sound of a bee**.

If you have not become tired and lost your physical power and if after a long time the pleasure is not complete, you should do the action of the movement of a swing if the thrills of passion can be borne. Through only shaking and stirring there is no certainty that an unfamiliarized person will have complete satisfaction, but as it can scratch the important spots of internal itching, it is seen that most women like this quintessential instruction.

---

[1] Presumably, the woman is sitting on the man's lap as in the previous posture.

One is an external sense organ.
The other is an internal hole of the body.
As red flesh and sinews are different,
How could the thorn know the feeling of a
　wound!

Find release at the great binding thighs.
Press with weight the great door of the lower
　parts where three roads meet.
Put the red top-ornament of coral with burning
　head inside,
And do it to the place of sacrament bestowing
　pleasure on a woman.

With both organs working tightly, the man moves his
hinder parts right and left; the phallus presses the
vagina like churning butter. This is called **churning**, *manthana*.

Sometimes take hold of the root of the phallus with a
hand and move it around inside the vagina. It is
medicine to clear away the pangs of passion; it should
especially be done to the dripping type. First put it in
straight; then at the finish of one pressing, press it upwards one, two, three, four times. Again two or three
times take it out and put it in. This is the **flapping of
birds**.

The woman puts her thighs together and forcefully
stretches out her legs. The man climbs on like a frog. He
pushes hard with his phallus like a mystical dagger. This
is called **very powerful**, *hula*, and should be done especially for the hard type.

Like a plow plowing the earth, the man moves his
rear up and down so that his phallus parts her vagina,
above and below. This is called **lustful pangs**, *sititaka*.

Like a male donkey putting it in from the rear, the
mouth of the vagina and the root of his sex sign meet;
he presses hard and for a long time. This is called **intoxicating**.

Like the deed of a bull and cow, enter to the mouth-door of the vagina right and left. Press it inside and shake the tip upwards. Both hit against each other's lower parts. This is called **motion of a bull**, *vṛṣa*.

Like the copulation of a horse and mare, pull the phallus a long way outside; then with the sound of ripples meet all the way to the root. The male hits, and the female leans against him. This is called **motion of a horse**, *aśva*.

Like the deed of a boar to a sow, gently, gently draw it upwards. When it arrives at the root, push hard and shake; touch, touch the mouth of the womb with the tip. This is called **motion of a boar**, *varāha*.

Then when tired, both touch forehead to forehead and rest. Again, with the earlier order perform the play of pleasure until satisfaction.

> The necklace of the early clouds of hope and
>   doubt diminish at midnight.
> Melt the moon of the self-arisen basic constituent
>   into milk. [1]
> Give young ladies the great spacious bliss,
> Clear and non-conceptual.

The above are the activities of moving to and fro and pressing.

---

[1] The male's seminal fluid is considered to be in a cold state at the top of the head and thus is compared to the moon; through sexual activities it is melted and flows downward.

13 Erotic Noises

When a focal point of passion is hit, like being hit on the chest with cold water the sound "hoo" of fright will suddenly come forth from a woman. Cold breaths, poo, poo, will come out. Sometimes it will be the wordless groan of the stupid and sometimes clear expressive cries. From the burning brighter of the activities of passion there are eight unusual sounds of birds.

(1) He beats her rear with the pangs of passion. She embraces him and puts her mouth to his; from inside the throat she emits the sound "noo".[1] This sound is called **voice of a pigeon**.

(2) The deeply penetrating tip of the jewel touches the tip of the womb. With passion like that from a spark she lets out the sound "hoo".[2] It is the **voice of a** *kokila*[3]

---

[1] *nūd*.

[2] *hud*.

[3] The 1983 edition (70.2) reads *kokki la*; the 1967 edition (89.8) reads *kaukki la*. In an interlinear note Gedün Chöpel identifies the bird as the Tibetan *khu byug* (cuckoo).

(cuckoo). The tone of that bird is choked, thin, and sorrowful.

(3) With strong pangs of unbearable passion she makes unclear crying noises and shouts as if falling down a ravine. This is called **voice of a peacock**. The tone of that bird is like the sound of a cat.

(4) Having swooned with the sleep of unspeakable bliss and dreaming of the sky and the earth copulating, she lets out a hissing sound, "sa si".[1] It is the **pleasant tone of a bee's sucking honey**.

(5) When the skin of timidity is pierced through and through with the sharp needle of passion difficult to endure, she cries, "Pleasure, wealth,"[2] for the sake of being pressed hard. The low sound of a bell, this is called **voice of a goose**.

(6) When the root of the phallus has entered the lotus [vagina], having become completely intoxicated and with confused clamor, she cries, "Salvation, wealth,"[3] so that it will be pulled out. Such is called **voice of a quail**, *lavaka*.

(7) Ravenous for the taste of passion unsatisfiable by the touch of joining the sex organs with no space between, she cries, "This is the meaning!"[4] for the sake of being pressed. This is said to be the **voice of a black goose**.

(8) Because with strong pleasure he moves forcefully with every entry and withdrawal, she cries, "The

---

[1] *za zi.*

[2] *śāta artha.*

[3] *mokṣa artha.*

[4] Following the 1967 edition (90.10) which reads *a ya marth*, which most likely is *ayamartha*; thanks to Professor David White for the translation. The 1983 edition (70.16) reads *a ma mārtha.*

ultimate!"[1] This is the **voice of a dove**.[2] Its tone resounds across all boundaries.

> By being pressed with strong force, satisfaction is
>   produced.
> Though pained by the fire of desire, bliss is ig-
>   nited.
> Though crying with unbearable groans, pleasure
>   is generated.
> O the great nature of amazing bliss!

The above was the making of erotic noises.

---

[1] *paramārtha.*

[2] In an interlinear note Gedün Chöpel glosses *thi ba* as *ti ti pho mo* (1967 edition: 90.14); the 1983 edition (70.19) reads *ti ti pho pho.*

14 The Deeds of the Man Done by the Woman

The woman plants her two feet at the man's armpits and, with her head facing downward [toward his feet], mounts. She bends her upper body and with her right and left hands holds onto the tops of his feet. Then she revolves her midriff to the front and to the outside. She pulls his phallus upward and enters it underneath; she revolves it around the right, left, front, and back sides of her vagina like a piece of wood. This gives pleasure to a young man with a hard phallus and to a passionate woman.

The man lies on his back on a bed as wide as his body or on long narrow pillows piled under his shoulders. The woman, like before, mounts but with front and back reversed. She puts the phallus in her vagina and brings her feet down on the right and left sides to the floor. Then, like before, the woman revolves her midriff. Sometimes she shifts to her front side and mounts.

Both stay squatting on a mattress. The left thigh of the woman is pressed by the thigh of the man, and the left thigh of the man is pressed by the thigh of the woman. With the lower part of their bodies a little crooked they meet; they embrace each other with the top leg. From time to time they shift the thigh on top to the bottom. Using this sexual embrace as a basis, other methods, lying and standing, are also similar.

The man puts his rear on a seat with the soles of his feet on the ground; the woman rises up on his lap, and they both embrace. She puts her two feet behind the man. Holding her waist with his two arms, he raises her upwards and presses her downwards. From time to time she rotates her rear without entering and pulling out, gently stirring her vagina. Certain passionate women of the country of Persia[1] are satisfied only through this method of union. It is called scented garden.[2] In the Arbhi [Arabic?] language this is known as *kelaka*.[3]

Men who have little strength, are tired, or are fat, as well as women whose passion is very great, do this type of deed with the woman mounting on top of the man. This is known as the woman's doing the work of the man. Old men in India take a young wife and, because they are unable to perform the tasks of the midriff, mostly follow this custom. It is a common custom in many areas.

(1) The man lies down; he spreads his thighs, and stretches his legs. The woman lies on top of him with her calves together. They meet at the root with her thighs and vagina closed. Hugging his shoulders with her arms, she rotates her rear and vibrates strongly. This is known as **way of a mare.**

(2) Mount like that, or mount as on a horse. The

---

[1] *par sig yul.*

[2] *dri zhim skyed tshal.*

[3] *ar bhi'i skad du sgrog kel a kar grags.* For discussion of this passage, see the note in the corresponding section of Chapter Four of the Introduction.

mouth of the vagina and the root of his sex sign meet. With their lower parts pressing hard, they embrace. Do not perform the work of entering in and pulling out [for the time being]. Then the woman completely rotates her rear alternately to the right and left and up and down. This is called **bee**, *bhramaraka*; it is known as **way a bee draws out honey**.

(3) Like the centers of mill-stones,[1] the tip of the phallus stirs about and rotates in the hole of the vagina. The man lies down, and the woman gets on his pubic region. She stretches out her two legs to the sides of his chest. They join hands and move like a swing. This is called **dwelling on a boat**.

(4) Above the man lying down, the woman puts her feet and hands on the ground and, bending, mounts. With every entry and withdrawal she looks at his long bulbous sex sign entering inside her. This is the act of an intoxicated girl; it is called **going and coming**, *gatāgata*.

(5) The woman sits on the man's pubic region. She stretches out her legs to his armpits. She puts her hands on the ground to the sides. They do whatever is pleasurable—the movement of a pestle or the movement of a swing. This is called **sound of a bed**.

(6) The woman wraps her two legs around the man; they join chests, and she embraces his shoulders. The man lies on his back with his upper body leaning on a pillow. This is called **opposite method**, *rodhanika*. They use both the pestle and the swing modes.

(7) With [their two organs] meeting well, the two legs of the male embrace the back of the female just as the female did. This is known as **way of taking hold of a pouch**. As entering and pulling out is difficult, use the movement of a swing. Also for other amazing methods

---

[1] Of the two mill-stones the one on the bottom has a protrusion in the middle and the one on the top has a hollow; these keep them in place when turning.

of copulation the swing method is just thoroughly pleasurable.

(8) The man lies down on his back and spreads his
thighs. He contracts his knees strongly. The woman
puts her midriff on his pubic region and puts her two
feet to the right and left of the man. Leaning back on
the thighs of the man, the woman does the work of entering and pulling out. With this method the phallus enters deep inside and again and again touches the door of
the womb. For this reason it is prohibited for pregnant
women. This is called **opposite method**, *rodhanika*.

A male has a little of the nature of a female, and a female has a little of the nature of a male. When mounting
on a man, if she has not seen it before, she will look
surprised. However, it is good to avoid this method if
the couple is seeking to have a baby or if the woman is
pregnant.

These methods of sex, shifting from top to bottom,
are for young women intoxicated with passion. In
Malaya[1] and so forth women are accustomed to this
and, though honored with gold, will not lie underneath.

The above was [the woman's doing] the activities of
the man.

---

[1] According to Professor David White, this is likely the region of
Kerala, sometimes called Malaya-deśa where Malayalam is spoken.

15 Methods of Copulation

(1) The woman, showing her back, rises on the lap of the man. She spreads her buttocks to the outside, and man and woman meet from their pubic regions. One hand of the man holds a breast of the woman, and the other squeezes from the side of the vagina. He hugs her moderately and enters and pulls out gently. Sometimes the woman should press a hand against a wall, and while doing the deed he should rub her labia with a finger. Similarly, if the underneath of the cheeks and the roots of the thighs and so forth are gently rubbed, immeasurable pleasure is produced.

(2) The woman lies down on her side and pushes her midriff to the rear. The man lies down behind her and joins to her vagina. He enters his head under her bosom and kisses and rubs a breast.

The man leans back on a bed[1]; the woman sets her midriff sideways, and they join. Her two legs are

---

[1] It is unclear whether the author considers this a separate posture or a continuation of the former one.

stretched out to the left over the man's thighs. One of her arms embraces the man's neck.

(3) The woman lies down on her back with a cushion under her rear. Her two feet are raised into the air with a rope of cloth. The man kneels and joins. For a while after the deed, leave the woman staying like that; it is said to aid conception a great deal.

(4) The man leans back on a bed and stretches his legs well in front. He spreads his thighs and sets his rear on the edge of a cushion. The woman, showing her back, comes onto his lap. She extends her posterior outside and puts the phallus into the vagina. Her two feet press against the bottom of a wall, and she presses her vagina hard on his pubic region. The woman rubs and rotates with her rear. Sometimes she presses her two hands against a railing in front of her and also does the work of entering in and pulling out. Otherwise, she can press her hands against a railing and just press against the root of the phallus as before. Shifting various heights of platforms, they do it. The moving to and fro and pressing is mainly done by the woman.

(5) The woman kneels on a cushion. She arches her midriff and spreads her buttocks outwards. The man spreads his thighs and does the deed from the rear. This is called **milk cow**, *dhenuka*. He extends his hand over a leg and rubs again and again the bulbous [vagina].

Another form of that is for the woman to stand bent; her two hands press against a bed or a corner. She arches her midriff and always stretches her posterior out to the rear. Women who have strong passion say that among the methods of copulation this is supreme. In many areas this is a common custom.

Another form of this is for the woman to kneel on a cushion as before. She arches her midriff and rests her upper parts on a slightly high cushion. Both male and female press each other. The man embraces her with an arm around her front and rubs her stomach upwards.

(6) The woman places her two hands behind her and, lying down on her back, presses her rear on the male. They meet from the rear and do the action of a swing. This intoxicates them a great deal, bestowing the tastes of pleasure. The man stretches out his legs under the thighs of the woman from the back toward the front. From time to time the woman turns her midriff to the side and stretches her two legs out on the man's left. Similarly, sometimes she changes to the right side. This is a good method to prevent pregnancy. All standing and sitting methods of copulation are also helpful in this regard.

(7) Placing her posterior on a platform, she touches her feet to the floor and spreads her legs. She stretches high her upper parts. The man rises from the front and joins her. This and other such methods of union are also very helpful for preventing pregnancy. In short, all methods of union (1) in which the reproductive organ is pointed downward and the phallus goes under the vagina and (2) in which the waist of the woman is not bent forward are helpful for preventing pregnancy. As soon as the seminal fluid has come out, the woman should rise and pound the floor with her heel. She should wash her vagina with warm water; it is the same as medicine for the prevention of pregnancy.

(8) Putting a cushion under her navel, she lies face down on a mat with her arms and legs stretched out. The man spreads his thighs and mounts from the rear. He puts a cheek to the center of her back. His two hands pull from the roots of her thighs at the knees, and, joining her rear to his midriff, he does it. Sometimes with the fingers of the right and left hands he squeezes the labia and presses. Alternating this and the other methods of copulation from the rear, do it.

She stretches her posterior outwards and shakes, rubbing and stroking the hollows of his stomach. Having bent his head down, he kisses her rear.

Likewise, he sucks the sides of her stomach and rubs with his tongue her armpits and under her breasts. Applying various intoxicating methods according to the feeling of the occasion, do it.

Because with play from the rear the labia are touched and rubbed, arousal is high; therefore, it can satisfy with passionately strong pleasure and, moreover, can especially bestow bliss on a woman. Those methods of copulation moving in from the rear are very helpful for impregnation. If she conceives during these, it is said the son born will be extraordinary.

> The glory of the essence achieved from one's
> 　own indestructible nature,
> The taste of honey born from the self-arisen
> 　body,
> This feeling from the play of a hundred thousand
> 　hairs,
> The tongues of gods in heavens have not tasted.
>
> By doing it with as many ways as there are, what
> 　can an old man say!
> How can those who do all of these secretly find
> 　blame!
> Though there are many forms of passion in the
> 　realm of desire,
> There is none surpassing the pubic region of a
> 　woman.

Those are various methods of copulation.

16 Uncertain Acts

The quintessential fluid in which the warmth of bliss does not diminish is the ambrosia of life for living beings. It is claimed[1] that though only a drop goes inside, it exceeds a hundred superior medicinal essences.

With pillows for his rear and his head, the man lies down from the end of a bed. The woman mounts him according to the opposite method [i.e., with the head toward the feet]. With thighs and cheeks touching, they join in that position. Through sucking and moving their tongues, strong bliss burns simultaneously in both for a long time. In whisper, this is called *mukhamaithuna* [oral union]. By another name it is the **wheel of whirling pleasure**; [pleasure] is twofold, threefold, tenfold, even many-fold.[2]

---

[1] Through a grammatically unsuitable ending (*go lo*) Gedün Chöpel indicates his disagreement with this assertion.

[2] Gedün Chöpel adds an interlinear note:

It is also called climbing aboard (*steng 'gyogs*) or *auparistaka*.

In the 1983 edition (80.16) for *steng mgyogs* read *steng 'gyogs* as in the

At the time of pleasure the god and goddess giving rise to bliss actually dwell in the bodies of the male and the female. Therefore, it is said that what would be ob-stacles to one's life if done [under usual circumstances] are conquered, and power, brilliance, and youth blaze forth. The perception of ugliness and dirtiness is stopped, and one is freed from conceptions of fear and shame. The deeds of body, speech, and mind become pure, and it is said that one arrives in a place of extreme pleasure.

The women of the West are greatly acquainted [with oral sex] nowadays. Previously in the country of India this was prevalent.[1] Most of the old temples of the Brahmins are full of such images.

By doing unsuitable deeds, sexual passion increases like a summer lake. However, with a woman who is unacquainted with them and thus embarrassed, these unusual methods are completely prohibited.

An ancient scripture says that whatever comes from the body of a woman during copulation is clean.[2] It is said that a Brahmin, while copulating, should drink the beer of the mouth of a woman until satisfaction. In an-other place it is said that demi-gods are born from blood. [However] even the mere taste of beer is the destroyer of one's lineage!

1967 edition (103.6), which, however, treats the line not as an inter-linear note but as part of the text.

Bhattacharya (88) and others translate *aupariṣṭaka* as "oral union". For *aupariṣṭa* Apte (321) gives "Being or produced above," and hence the Tibetan *steng*.

[1] Gedün Chöpel adds an interlinear note:

During the eras of the lineage of Gupta Kings and so forth.

[2] Gedün Chöpel cites the scripture in an interlinear note:

Birds when flying, dogs when hunting, and calves when sucking milk are clean, and likewise [whatever comes from the body of a woman during copulation is clean].

The vagina of a desired girl is the mouth of Brahmā, bestowing body and bliss on embodied beings. Getting satisfaction from the deed of another is the magic of Rāma, the god of wealth. So it is claimed.[1]
For those intoxicated by inexhaustible pleasure in whom the fiery tongue of bliss vibrates inside—the essential fluid having been bound in the thousand channels—there are no prohibitions.

> Looking at a mirror in front, do it.
> Squeezing a nipple with the teeth, suck.
> With the tongue clean away the dripping feminine fluid,[2] and so forth.
> Intoxicated and confusing the memory, do everything.

> Smear honey on each other and taste.
> Or taste the natural fluids.
> Suck the slender and bulbous tube.[3]
> Intoxicated and confusing the memory, do everything.

> Tell risqué stories.
> Reveal completely the hidden places.
> Think and do embarrassing things.
> Intoxicated and without analysis, do everything.

These deeds [of oral sex] are described in the treatises of Female Sky Travelers[4] for the sake of satisfying extremely passionate men and women who can hold the

---

[1] Through a grammatically unsuitable ending (*pa lo*) Gedün Chöpel indicates his disagreement.

[2] The 1983 edition (82.5) reads *raṇḍa*; *raṇḍā* means whore but is meaningless here. The 1967 edition (105.3) reads *rakta*, which means blood, the essential feminine element.

[3] *nali*. Apte identifies *nāli* (543) as "any tubular vessel of the body".

[4] *mkha' 'gro ma, ḍākiṇī*. These are beings especially dedicated to assisting in the practice of tantra.

constitutional essences in their bodies without emission.[1]

> When the self-arisen blood [the female essence]
>   goes inside the man
> And when the essence of the moon [the male
>   essence] dissolves inside a woman,
> Superior power and bliss are definitely achieved.
> They become like Shaṃkara[2] and Uma.

Those are the uncertain[3] acts.

---

[1] This is the tantric practice of orgasm without emission.

[2] Another name for Shiva.

[3] They are uncertain in the sense of being restricted, or not definite for all persons.

17 Helpful Techniques

The following are techniques of pleasure posited for powerful men and passionate women so that they may sustain mental deeds, according to wish, upon entering the wheel of intrepid desire. One should use a method of sex suitable for the occasion, having understood well the customs of various areas and the different constitutions of individual women.

Those who have just given birth, those suffering in pregnancy, those who are ill, those with great worry, and those who are very old or very young are never suitable for the deeds of passion.

Through cleverly using various arts, jokes, conversation of passion, touching, kissing, and other appropriate methods, tame the proud and embarrassed. For a woman of the lotus type, prepare a atmosphere of peace: cover soft cushions with a white cloth; place vessels of fragrant waters nearby; and arrange bunches of small flowers. For a woman of the picture type, prepare an atmosphere of beauty: cover a bouncy bed with a multiolored cloth; also arrange various pictures; and place edibles like honey and so forth nearby. For a woman of the conch type, prepare an atmosphere of

wealth: cover the bed with deer skin, smooth and supple; surround it with cushions of various sizes; and place
lovely sounding musical instruments there. Play with a
woman of the elephant type in an atmosphere of
power: place a hard mattress with thin cushions on a
bed surrounded by darkness; and nearby place foods
that are aphrodisiacs, like the meat of fish.

The vagina of women of Āryan lineage is high to -
ward the stomach. They give birth with difficulty and
with great pain. It is most suitable to use methods of
front copulation.

The women of the Maugal lineage have big ab-
domens, and their vaginas are near their rears. Even
youths of this type easily give birth to children.
Methods of rear copulation are very appropriate.

A woman who has thick buttocks has by nature a
high vagina. Having stretched out his two legs with
force on the mattress the man should mount from the
top and do it.

Similarly, whatever woman has a large stomach has
by nature a low vagina. Having placed cushions under
her rear, the man should raise her feet to her shoulders
and do it.

A woman whose right and left cheeks are full with
little scaliness[1] has a deep hairless round hole. Her labia
are hard, and her lotus through which a central nerve
passes is said to be produced from water.

The scaliness of another's mouth is thick, and her two
cheeks are low. She has bristly hair, and her feminine
secretion flows warm. Her inner passage is narrow, and
her lotus which grasps the tip of the phallus is said to be
produced from mud.

The door of another's vagina is narrow, generating
pain. Great warmth burns, and it is rough like the

---

[1] The translation of *shun bu* (1983 edition, 84.18 here and in the next
paragraph is doubtful.

tongue of a bull. Her secretion is slight. This lotus which makes the phallus swell is said to be produced from dry earth.

Whoever has red eyes with orange pupils, thick lips with upper lip curled upwards, a space between her front teeth, and red gums is a passionate woman.

If the tip of her nose points downward, the blood vessels on her forehead show when laughing, and the center of her face is bent with a high center, she has signs of being passionate.

Whoever is seen to have prominent eyes, red cheeks, fine wrinkles in the center of her ears, and whose stomach, upper thighs, and calves are large has signs of great passion.

Whoever shifts her head when she is looked at straightway, who closes her lips again and again when talking, and who has the design of a lotus around her lips has signs of great passion and a good vagina.

On the first three days of menstruation a woman should stay alone in a solitary place. On the fourth day she should wash her body and massage it well with fragrant oil. If on these days she copulates, it is a very unsuitable low act.

If she becomes pregnant on the fifth, seventh, ninth, eleventh, thirteenth, and fifteenth days after menstruating, she will have a daughter, and hence it is suitable to avoid copulation on those days. If from sleeping with a man on the sixth, eighth, tenth, twelfth, and fourteenth days she conceives, the child born will be a boy.

If she conceives on the fifth day, she will give birth to a girl who will attain only ordinary prosperity.

If she conceives on the sixth day, she will give birth to a boy who will live only by way of low work.

If she conceives on the seventh day, she will give birth to a girl, who will have a religious mind and will always be happy.

If she conceives on the eighth day, she will give birth

to a boy who will know various sciences and will attain fame.

She who conceives on the ninth day will definitely have a girl who will be very attractive like Gandarvī.

She who conceives on the tenth day will give birth to a heroic learned boy, who will attain the glory of religion conquering all.

Whoever conceives on the eleventh day will give birth to a beautiful intelligent girl.

Whoever conceives on the twelfth day will give birth to a boy who will have youthful power and will conquer over his enemies.

She who conceives on the thirteenth day will have a girl with little passion or selfishness and with respect for religion.

She who conceives on the fourteenth will give birth to a boy who will undergo many effects of ill-deeds.[1]

She who conceives on the fifteenth day will give birth to a girl who has a good body but will suffer various miseries.

Conceived on the sixteenth day is a boy who will be clever and courageous and will obtain much wealth.

The eighth day of the month as well as the fourteenth, the fifteenth, the first, the thirtieth, and so forth are auspicious times of charity and worship. As all the gods deride it, give up sleeping together on those days. If a woman conceives at those times, her children will be vicious and fierce. Similarly, it is said that if one copulates on the last day of the year and during eclipses etc., [the child] will die.

A woman's craving for sex is very strong for two or three months after conceiving. It is also very strong when, after giving birth, the purificatory rites have been performed and she is free from sickness and also when

---

[1] In the 1983 edition (87.7) read '*thob par 'gyur* for *thos par 'gyur* in accordance with the 1967 edition (111.12).

a day has passed after finishing menstruation. If while the man is nearby he does not do it with his wife, he will go to a fearful hell upon dying since he abandons the better teachings of behavior for men.

The days appropriate for lying together as prescribed by the ancient sages are these. Many scholars have said that most of the fruits of timeliness are just inevitable. In particular, from the cessation of menstruation to the eighth day afterward, the mouth of the womb is open, due to which conception is definite. Though conception could occur after the eighth day, with most women the door of the womb has closed.

Before copulation both the male and the female should clean away all excretions and wash their sexual organs. Especially the recesses of the vagina should be cleansed; this helps conception in flawless wombs.

If during union fright, anxiety, and so forth arise, harm will occur later to the womb; therefore, it is very important to have sex in a solitary place, relaxed and without any apprehension. Afterward,[1] while the man stops his left nostril and breathes through the right, the woman should lie down on her left side and the man on his right and sleep for a while.

If [a couple] wishes to have a boy, the female[2] should raise strong passion for the male. The male should imagine himself as a woman or strive at methods of slow and weak passion. Similarly, if [a couple] wishes to have a girl, the male should generate strong passion for the female; the female should stay without paying attention, and he should strongly emit a great deal of seminal fluid. This is the essence of an extremely important essential; the child's becoming male or female

---

[1] In the 1983 edition (88.16) read *de nas* for *des nas* in accordance with the 1967 edition (113.9).

[2] In the 1983 edition (89.1) read *mo yis* for *mo yi* in accordance with the 1967 edition (113.14).

depends on this. A passionate woman gives birth to many boys; a passionate man definitely has daughters. Therefore, it is a mistake to think that if the passion of the male is more powerful, a male child will be conceived.

The mother's disposition, constitution, physical strengths, and so forth all come to the continuums of her sons. Likewise, the father's disposition, physical constitution, and so forth all definitely arise in the continuums of his daughters.

After finishing the deed, the woman should not rise immediately; she should put a pillow under her rear and sleep. Then having drunk milk and so forth, it is good for them to sleep separately on their own beds.

During the first copulation the man by nature has stronger passion; hence when the seminal fluid is emitted, he should pull out and let it go on the outside of the vagina. During the second copulation the woman's passion is ignited; therefore, the seed should be emitted in the vagina. If she is impregnated with such a technique, it definitely helps toward getting a male child.

If both become intoxicated through strong passion, as the woman's passion is by nature stronger, the child produced will most likely be a male. However, [the rising of their passion] must be simultaneous. In short, until a mind of strong passion has been produced in the woman by various arts of passion, it helps important essentials not to lie together [i.e., it helps to put off copulation].

It is said that the sense that all of one's insides are filled with various types of filth, loss of appetite, and the dripping of water and mucous from the mouth are signs of having become pregnant. If a pregnant woman has strong desire for copulation, it is a sign the child dwelling in the womb is a girl.

Then always avoid causes producing fear, like looking down deep caverns or wells. If copulation can be given up, it is good. If it cannot, use methods of union from the side. If the stomach is pressed or the like when the womb has filled out, the limbs of the child will degenerate. In particular, as a thumb of the child stays around the nose, there is great danger of developing a hare lip.

During birth, an experienced woman should be nearby. Gently rub and squeeze the abdomen downwards. Then, when the child arrives at the door of the female organ, by squeezing strongly, it will come out easily. If the baby is obstructed at the door of the womb, fumigate with the skin of a black snake. Through stretching out the two arms and shaking them, the placenta will emerge. Then when the next menstruation occurs, it is said that the process of birth has been purified.[1]

> Though there are many sufferings hard to endure,
> There is no bliss harder to bear other than this.
> If one were able to stop the day of the full moon,
> There would be no way for there to be darkness until the day of the new moon.[2]

If one does not know the techniques of holding and spreading the bliss that has arrived at the tip of the jewel [i.e., the head of the phallus], immediately upon seeing it for a moment it fades and disappears, like picking up a snowflake in the hand. Therefore when, upon churning about, bliss is generated, cease movement, and again and again spread [the sense of bliss throughout the body]. Then, by again doing it with the former methods, bliss will be sustained for a long time.

From time to time, both should wipe the private parts

---

[1] Translation doubtful; the Tibetan (1983 edition, 91.5) reads *btsas pa'i bang sangs nyid du brjod par bya.*

[2] Translation doubtful; the Tibetan (1983 edition, 91.7) reads *zla ba nya yi nyin mo 'gog nus na/ /gnam stong bar du mun pa yong don med.*

well with a clean cloth. Then do it, shifting among various methods of copulation, and the bliss will become very powerful. Hold the seminal fluid a long time by looking with eye and mind at a spot in the middle of the woman's brow and at her face and by strongly asking and answering words of passion.

When the fluid arrives at the root of the male sign, the lower parts become heavy and numb; hence, at that time imagine the expanse of the sky and pull inward strongly, whereby its reversal will be certain. Close the lower gate [the anus], and turn the tongue and eyes upwards. Contract the joints of the feet and hands, and tighten the fingers strongly. Pull in the stomach to the backbone. These are physical techniques that should be done.

Aim the mind at the multiplication table—eight times three is twenty-four, six times five is thirty, and so forth. Also, if the woman pinches him and emphatically says, "Look here," he will be able to bind the seminal fluid.

If when bliss spreads throughout the body, one can stop the attention from going to the lower parts and can experience with the mind the feeling of bliss only of the upper body, the regenerative fluid will not diminish no matter how much one plays. . The causes and conditions of losing the seminal fluid derive from not experiencing in a broad and vast way the bliss fully pervading the body and, instead of that, aiming the mind to the bliss of only the private parts.

> As much as one approaches the nature of a thing,
> So much do the words of scholars become dumb.
> Hence it is said that by nature all subtle phenomena
> Pass beyond proposition, thought, and verbalization.
>
> Having set the mind in the realm of emptiness endowed with all aspects,

Who could view[1] this wheel of illusory appear-
ances
With a mind of asserting is and is not
That even the hand of Buddha[2] does not prevent!

The small child of intelligence swoons in the deep
sphere of passion.
The busy mind falls into the hole of a worm.
By drawing the imaginations of attachment
downwards
Beings should observe the suchness of pleasure.

Wishing to mix in the ocean of the bliss of the
peaceful expanse
This wave of magician's illusions separated off
By perceiving the non-dual as dual, subject and
object,
Does one not feel the movement and igniting of
the coalesced![3]

To what could this reality devoid of projection
move?
Where could this mind devoid of pursuit run?
Since, having abandoned their nature, they do
not stay still,
Move these two—appearances and mind—in the
direction of bliss.

Even taking a single step is for the sake of seeking bliss.
Even speaking a single word is for the sake of
seeking bliss.

---

[1] In the 1983 edition (93.4) read *mthong* for *thong* in accordance with
the 1967 edition (118.20).

[2] Literally, One Gone Thus (*de bzhin gshegs pa, tathāgata*).

[3] The translation of the last line of this stanza follows the usually
unreliable 1967 edition (119.8) which more comprehensibly reads '*du
'khrig g.yo zhing 'bar ba ma tshor ram*; the 1983 edition (93.9) reads
'*du 'phrig g.yo zhing 'phar ba ma tshor ram*.

Virtuous deeds are done for the sake of bliss.
Non-virtuous deeds also are done for the sake of
    bliss.

Eyeless ants run after bliss.
Legless worms run after bliss.
In short, all worldly beings one by one
Are running, faster and slower, in the direction of
    bliss.

If one really considers the fact that the one billion
    worlds of this world system
Are suddenly swallowed into a gigantic asteroid
    devoid of perception or feeling,
One understands that the realm of great bliss
Is that in which all appearances dissolve.

Though they have attained the glory and wealth
    of the three billion worlds, they are not satis-
    fied
And therefore come to be renowned for burning
    ravenous passion.
In fact they seek the sky-kingdom of bliss and
    emptiness
With the dumb child of a mind knowing noth-
    ing.[1]

---

[1] Gedün Chöpel adds an interlinear note:

The easy-to-understand explanation of the union of the
two—bliss and emptiness—in the manner of subject and object varies greatly from the thought of the tantras. Therefore,
here regarding the inexpressible meaning that is the final nature of the stable [environment] and moving [living beings],
when one considers it from a negative viewpoint it is empty,
and when it dawns from a positive viewpoint, it is bliss.
Emptiness is a non-affirming negative, and bliss is positive,
whereby one may wonder how granting the two of these to
one base could be suitable, but one should not fear any reasonings that put their stock in dualistic conceptions.

18 Conclusion

Obeisance to the god of self-arisen pleasure,
Though uncharacterizable, having the aspect of
   characteristics,
Teaching the pure reality to superior beings,
And jesting with the children of darkness.

Obeisance to the god of self-arisen pleasure.
Vivid to those without meditation and to the
   minds of the stupid,
You accompany all and all are your companion,
Seen by all but known by no one.

Obeisance to the god of self-arisen pleasure,
Spatial entertainer not covered with the clothes
   of the conventional,
Having countless magical forms without color
   and shape,
Flinging the shooting star of consciousness experienced but not grasped.

Obeisance to the great self-arisen bliss
Where the rainbow lights of the varieties of elab-
    orations dissolve,
Devoid of the waves of the ocean of magical illu-
    sions,
Where the fluctuating mind does not fluctuate.

Obeisance to the sphere of self-arisen bliss,
Seen by the eyes of Buddhas that never close,
Experienced by the educated upon the severance
    of propositional statements,
Comprehended by a non-grasping mind through
    the non-elaboration of conceptions.

Here [in this book] there has been no proclamation of
the secret—the profound modes of practice, the vocabulary, and so forth of Secret Mantra. Nevertheless, with
diligence embarrassing deeds should just be kept secret
from others.

Since monks, Foe Destroyers,[1] elders, and Solitary
Realizers are not intended to read this text, it is right for
them only to read the title and set it aside rather than
raising shame and anger from reading it well. The natures of worldly beings are different; their thoughts and
conceptions do not agree. Therefore, some will blame
and some will praise it; some will consider it dirty and
some will consider it clean.

It would be better for the carnivorous wolf and the
grass-eating rabbit, rather than comparing each other's
advice on the topic of food, to further their own individual style of behavior among agreeable companions
of similar type. There is no sense in urgently exhorting
people to do what they do not wish—[asking] nomads
to eat pork, city-folk to drink melted butter, and so on.
There is also no sense in strictly preventing what one
desires. The good and bad, the clean and the dirty are

---

[1] *dgra bcom pa, arhan/arhat.*

only one's own fancy. One should proceed, always shifting among desired activities. Debating and arguing about these will only wear one out. Analyzing for rea-sons will eventually afflict [one's own mind].

Examining through one's own experience how much attitudes change from childhood through to the decrepi-tude of old age, how could confidence be put in current conceptions![1] Sometimes even looking at a goddess, one is disgusted; sometimes even looking at an old woman, passion is generated. Something exists now, but later it will not be, and something else will come. Number can-not encompass the deceptions of the mind. When such is understood well, the mind is cut off, and the root of considering the objects of the imagination to be real is destroyed. That is the great relief of bliss; another syn-onym is freedom.

The lake Manasarowara which is said to be huge by those who have not seen it is a bird's[2] puddle when one arrives nearby. When one bends and tastes the phe-nomena of cyclic existence, it is so true that there is no amazing essence. However, there are neither fewer nor more men than women, and each is easy to find. If one wishes the other, the sin of craving is greater than that of doing it. Hence, it is right to partake of the enjoy-ments of sex in all ways.

When experience has been gained over a long time, there is nothing that does not sadden the mind in terms of this lifetime. Relieving a saddened mind is the divine religion of the excellent. Eventually, it comes down to what is done with the mind.

The stupid who cherish unfabricated appearances and the clever who create fabricated imaginations split off

---

[1] This sentence (four lines of verse) is cited in Gedün Chöpel's *Ornament for the Thought of Nāgārjuna* (bod ljongs bod yig dpe rnying dpe skrun khang: 1990), 281.1.

[2] *ko mo.*

from discordant paths, but again at the end of the three paths[1] come together.

If, having seen the depths of the ocean of cyclic existence, one cannot bear the sadness due to wishing to leave it, one should take the life of a saffron-robed [monk or nun] and become solely absorbed in the doctrine of peace. Tibetan scholars in the good eras of yore came to India, the country of Superiors; they possessed the three learnings [of ethics, meditative stabilization, and wisdom] and bound the three doors [of body, speech, and mind with vows]. However, [nowadays] it is hard to bear even hearing talk about such.

I have little shame and great faith in women. From the past I indeed have not had a head for vows, the type who binds the bad and casts aside the good, but recently the entrails [i.e., even the remnants] of deception have ceased here [in India].[2]

> The acquaintance of a watery fish is profound
>   when it comes to water.
> One has more knowledge of what one has experienced.
> Thinking this, I wrote with hard work
> This treatise that is my lot.
>
> Derision by monks would not be unsuitable.

---

[1] The three times?

[2] Translated in accordance with the 1983 edition (98.2) which reads *sdom pa'i mgo bo sngon nas med mod kyang/ brdzu yi rgyu ma*. The 1967 edition (125.1) reads *sdom pa'i ngo bo sngon nas yod mod kyang/ brdzu yi sgyu ma* which in English would be:

> Though I formerly had the entity of vows, binding the bad and casting aside the good, this deception recently ceased here.

Both readings make sense, but since Gedün Chöpel was rebellious even when a monk, I prefer the reading of the 1983 edition which in almost all cases is superior to the 1967 edition.

Nor would praise by Tantric practitioners not be
   permitted.
[This book] is of little purpose for an old Lu-gyel-
   bum.[1]
It is of great purpose for a young Sö-nam-tar.
The author is Gedün Chöpel.
The place of composition is the city of Mathurā.
The explicator of difficult passages was an old
   Brahmin.
A Kashmiri girl gave naked instruction[2] in expe-
   rience.

The root of the explication runs back to Indian
   texts.
The verse was put together in the Tibetan style,
   easy to understand.
Hence I have the feeling that from the cause of its
   not being incomplete
It will definitely give rise to wonderful effects.

The venerable Mi-pam[3] wrote from having studied [these topics],
And the lascivious Chöpel[4] wrote from experience.

---

[1] *klu rgyal 'bum*. Stoddard (309, n. 58) reports that in the Am-do di-
alect Lu-gyel-bum and Sö-nam-tar (*bsod nams thar*) are stereotypical
patronymics. Thus, they are like Smith and Jones.

[2] *dmar khrid*. This term is used to refer a type of religious discourse,
in which "the words of a text are explained in terms of what they actually refer to, not merely in terms of their literal meaning." See
Gedün Lodrö, *Walking Through Walls: A Presentation of Tibetan
Meditation* (Ithaca: Snow Lion Publications, forthcoming). The pun
here is obvious.

[3] *mi pham/'ju mi pham rgya mtsho/mi pham 'jam dbyangs rnam rgyal*;
1846-1912. Mi-pam also wrote a *Treatise on Passion*, which can be
found in the back of the 1983 edition of Gedün Chöpel's work.

[4] The author, Gedün Chöpel.

That these two [treatises] differ in terms of their
impact will be known
By passionate males and females through putting
them into practice.

However, if it appears to be excessive to those
devoid of passion
Or appears to be too brief to passionate beings,
and so forth,
Thereby coming to have the faults of redundancy
or incompleteness,
I will confess it from my heart without conceal-
ment or hiding.

[However] do not put on a humble person's
head
One's own individual faults, like the destruction
Of the lifestyle of friends with proper behavior
Or the loss of composure of the pretentious, and
so forth.

Through this virtue[1] may all concordant friends
Cross the dark path of material desires
And from the mountain peak of the sixteen plea-
sures
See the sky of the meaning of reality.

May the girls who have physical connection with
me—
Yu-drön,[2] Gangā,[3] Asali, and so forth—

---

[1] The virtue of writing this book.

[2] *g.yu sgron.* Gedün Chöpel lived with a woman by this name after
being released from prison, but this could not be her (since he wrote
the treatise in India in 1938), unless he married someone he knew
earlier or if he added the conclusion to this work after being released from prison, as Stoddard (202) suggests. La-chung-a-po
(656.16) declares that this Yu-drön is not the one near the end of his
life.

[3] Most likely, this is Gangā Deva in whose home he finished the

Pass along the path from pleasure to pleasure
And arrive at the place of the Truth Body[1] of
   great bliss.

May all the humble who act on this broad earth
Have manifest freedom from the pit of merciless
   laws,
And in common be able to partake of small plea-
   sures,
Necessary and suitable, with independence.

This *Treatise on Passion* was written by Gedün Chöpel who passed to the far side of our own[2] and others'[3] topics of knowledge, like an ocean, and who eliminated false superimpositions with regard to sexual desire through[4] seeing, hearing, and experiencing. It was finished in the latter part of the middle month of winter in the Tiger Year [1938] near the shore of the glorious Yamunā River, endowed with the cast of a summer dawn, in the great city of Mathurā, Magadha, in the home of Gangā Deva from Pañcāla, girl-friend with the same life-style.

---

work. See the final paragraph.
[1] *chos sku, dharmakāya.*
[2] Buddhist.
[3] Non-Buddhist.
[4] In the 1983 edition (99.17) read *gsum gyis* for *gsum gyi* in accordance with the 1967 edition (127. 5).

Bibliography

Note: 'P', standing for 'Peking edition', refers to the *Tibetan Tripiṭaka* (Tokyo-Kyoto: Tibetan Tripiṭaka Research Foundation, 1956).

1. SŪTRA

Sūtra of Teaching to Nanda on Entry to the Womb
tshe dang ldan pa dga' bo mngal du 'jug pa bstan pa
āyuṣmannandagarbhāvakrāntinirdeśa
P760.13, vol. 23

2. OTHER WORKS

Agrawala, P. K. *The Unknown Kamasutras.* Varanasi: Books Asia, 1983.

Bhattacharya, Narendra Nath. *History of Indian Erotic Literature.* Munshiram Manoharlal Publishers Pvt. Ltd. (n.d.).

Burton, Sir Richard. *The Perfumed Garden.* Edited and introduced by Charles Fowkes. Rochester, Vermont: Park Street Press, 1989.

Cabezón, José Ignacio. *Buddhism, Sexuality, and Gender.* Albany: State University of New York Press, 1992.

Devarāja, *Ratiratnapradīpikā.* Ed. with English translation by K. Rangaswami Iyengar. Mysore: 1923.

Dhondup, K. "Gedun Chophel: the Man Behind the Legend". *Tibetan Review*, vol. xiii no. 10, October, 1978, 10-18.

Donden, Dr. Yeshi *Health Through Balance*. Ithaca: Snow Lion Publications, 1986.

Dorje, Rinjing. *Tales of Uncle Tompa, The Legendary Rascal of Tibet*. San Rafael, California: Dorje Ling, 1975.

Dre-tong Tup-den-chö-dar (*bkras mthong thub bstan chos dar*). *dge 'dun chos 'phel gyi lo rgyus*. Dharamsala: Library of Tibetan Works & Archives, 1980.

Choephel, Gedun. *The White Annals*, translated by Samten Norboo. Dharamsala: Library of Tibetan Works and Archives, 1978.

Chöpel, Gedün (*dge 'dun chos 'phel*). *dbu ma'i zab gdad snying por dril ba'i legs bshad klu sgrub dgongs rgyan* (*Good Explanation Distilling the Profound Essentials of the Middle: Ornament for the Thought of Nāgārjuna*). Kalimpong: Mani Printing Works, 1951; also: bod ljongs bod yig dpe rnying dpe skrun khang, 1990.

Chöpel, Gedün (*dge 'dun chos 'phel*). *'dod pa'i bstan bcos*. Delhi: T. G. Dhongthog Rinpoche, 1967; also an edited edition, Delhi: T. G. Dhongthog Rinpoche, 1969; reprinted without preface, Dharamsala: Tibetan Cultural Printing Press, 1983.

Das, Sarat Chandra. *A Tibetan-English Dictionary*. Calcutta, 1902.

Dzay-may Lo-sang-bel-den (*dze me blo bzang dpal ldan*). *'jam dpal dgyes pa'i gtam gyi rgol gnan phye mar 'thags pa'i reg chod ral gri'i 'khrul 'khor*. Delhi: 1972.

Dzong-ka-ba (*tsong kha pa*). *rten 'brel bstod pa/sangs rgyas bcom ldan 'das la zab mo rten cing 'brel bar 'byung ba gsung ba'i sgo nas bstod pa legs par bshad pa'i snying po* (*Praise of Dependent-Arising/ Praise of the Supramundane Victor Buddha from the Approach of His Teaching the Profound Dependent-Arising, The Essence of the Good Explanations*). P6016, vol. 153. English translations: Geshe Wangyal, *The Door of Liberation*, 117-25. New York: Lotsawa, 1978; Robert Thurman, *Life and Teachings of Tsong Khapa*, 99-107. Dharamsala: Library of Tibetan Works and Archives, 1982.

Goldstein, Melvyn C. *A History of Modern Tibet, 1913-1951; The Demise of the Lamaist State*. Berkeley: University of California Press, 1989.

Hopkins, Jeffrey. *Meditation on Emptiness*. London: Wisdom Publications, 1983.

Hopkins, Jeffrey. "Tantric Buddhism, Degeneration or Enhancement: the View of a Tibetan Tradition", *Buddhist-Christian Studies*, Vol. 10, 1990.

Jyotirīshvara, *Pañcasāyaka*. Ed. S. Shastri Ghiladia. Lahore: 1921.

Kalyāṇamalla, *Anaṅgaranga*.
English translations
Burton, Sir Richard and Arbuthnot, F. F. *The Ananga Ranga or the Hindu Art of Love of Kalyana Malla*. London: 1885; New York: G. P. Putnam's Sons, 1964.
Ray, T. L. *Ananga-Ranga*. Calcutta: Medical Book Agency, 1960.
Sanskrit editions
Bhandāri, Visnu-prasāda. *Kalyāṇa-malla: Anaṅga-Ranga*. Kashi Sanskrit Series No. 9. Benares: 1923.
R. Shastri Kusala. *Anaṅgaranga*. Lahore: 1890.

Karmay, Heather (alias Heather Stoddard). "dGe-'dun Chos-'phel, the artist" in *Tibetan Studies in Honour of Hugh Richardson*, ed. Michael Aris and Aung San Suu Kyi. Warminster, Wiltshire: Aris and Phillips Ltd., 1980.

Kokkoka, *Ratirahasya*.
English translations
Comfort, Alex. *The Koka Shastra, Being the Ratirahasya of Kokkoka, and Other Medieval Indian Writings on Love*. London: George Allen and Unwin, 1964.
Upadhyaya, S. C. *Kokashastra (Rati Rahasya) of Pandit Kokkoka*. Bombay: Taraporevala, 1965.
German translation
Leinhard, S. *Kokkoka-Ratirahasya*. Stuttgart: Franz Decker, 1960.
Sanskrit edition
S. S. Ghildiyāl. *Ratirahasya* (with Kāñcinātha's commentary). Lahore: Bombay Sanskrit Press, 1923.

Kṣemendra. *Kalāvilāsa*
Sanskrit edition
Kāvyamāla. 1888
German translation
Schmidt, Richard. Leipzig: 1914.

La-chung-a-po (*bla chung a pho*). *dge 'dun chos 'phel.* In *Biographical Dictionary of Tibet and Tibetan Buddhism,* compiled by Khetsun Sangpo, vol. 5, 634-657. Dharamsala: Library of Tibetan Works and Archives, 1973.

Lati Rinbochay and Jeffrey Hopkins. *Death, Intermediate State, and Rebirth in Tibetan Buddhism.* London: Rider, 1979; Ithaca: Snow Lion Publications, 1980.

Lodrö, Gedün. *Walking Through Walls: A Presentation of Tibetan Meditation.* Trans. and ed. by Jeffrey Hopkins. Co-edited by Anne C. Klein and Leah Zahler. Ithaca: Snow Lion Publications, 1992.

Lo-sang-chö-ḡyi-gyel-tsen, First Paṇ-chen Lama (*blo bzang chos kyi rgyal mtshan*). *rgyud thams cad kyi rgyal po bcom ldan 'das dpal dus kyi 'khor lo'i rtsa ba'i rgyud las phyung ba bsdus pa'i rgyud kyi rgyas 'grel dri ma med pa'i 'od kyi rgya cher bshad pa de kho na nyid snang bar byed pa'i snying po bsdus pa yid bzhin gyi nor bu* (Wish-Granting Jewel, Essence of (Kay-drup's) "Illumination of the Principles: Extensive Explanation of (Kulika Puṇḍarīka's) 'Extensive Commentary on the Condensed Kālachakra Tantra, Derived from the Root Tantra of hhe Supramundane Victor, the Glorious Kālachakra, the King of All Tantras: the Stainless Light'"). Collected Works of Blo-bzañ-chos-kyi-rgyal-mtshan, the First Pan-chen Bla-ma of Bkra-śis-lhun-po, vol. 3. New Delhi: Gurudeva, 1973.

Mi-pam-gya-tso (*mi pham rgya mtsho/mi pham 'jam dbyangs rnam rgyal*). *'dod pa'i bstan bcos 'jig rten kun tu dga' ba'i gter* (Treatise on Passion: Treasure Pleasing All the World). Delhi: T. G. Dhongthog Rinpoche, 1969; reprinted without preface, Dharamsala: Tibetan Cultural Printing Press, 1983.

Nāgārjuna and the Seventh Dalai Lama. *The Precious Garland and the Song of the Four Mindfulnesses.* New York: Harper and Row, 1975; rpt. in *The Buddhism of Tibet.* London: George Allen and Unwin, 1983, and Ithaca: Snow Lion Publications, 1987.

Nāgārjuna, Siddha. *Ratiśāstra.*
English translation
Ghose, A. C. *Ratiśāstra.* Calcutta: Seal, 1904.
Sanskrit edition
Richard Schmidt. "Das Ratiśāstra des Nāgārjuna" in *Wiener Zeitschrift fur die Kunde des Morgenlandes,* XXIII, 1909, pp. 180-183.

Roerich, George N. *The Blue Annals*. Delhi: Motilal Banarsidass, rpt. 1979.

Ruegg, D. Seyfort. "A Tibetan Odyssey: A Review Article". *Journal of the Royal Asiatic Society*, no. 2, 1989, pp.304-311.

Shay-rap-gya-tso (*shes rab rgya mtsho*). *klu sgrub dgongs rgyan la che long du brtags pa mi 'jigs sengge'i nga ro*. Collected Works, vol. 3, 1-246. Ch'inghai: mtsho sngon mi rigs dpe skrun khang, 1984.

Sopa, Geshe Lhundup, and Hopkins, Jeffrey. *Practice and Theory of Tibetan Buddhism*. London: Rider and Co., 1976; second edition: *Cutting Through Appearances: The Practice and Theory of Tibetan Buddhism*. Ithaca: Snow Lion, 1990.

Stoddard, Heather. *Le mendiant de L'Amdo*. Recherches sur la Haute Asie 9. Paris: Société d'Ethnographie, 1985.

Surūpa/or Abhirūpapāda (Tib. *gzugs bzang zhabs*). *'dod pa'i bstan bcos*. P3323, vol. 157, 31.5.2-33.1.1.

Thomas, P. *Kāma Kalpa or The Hindu Ritual of Love*. Bombay: D. B. Taraporevala, 1960, rpt. 1981.

Thurman, Robert, ed. *The Life & Teachings of Tsong Khapa*. Dharamsala: Library of Tibetan Works and Archives, 1982.

Tsong-ka-pa, Kensur Lekden, and Jeffrey Hopkins. *Compassion in Tibetan Buddhism*. London: Rider and Company, 1980; rpt. Ithaca: Snow Lion, 1980.

Vasubandhu. *Abhidharmakośakārikā*.
Sanskrit edition
P. Pradhan, ed. *Abhidharmakośabhāṣyam of Vasubandhu*. Patna: Jayaswal Research Institute, 1975.
Tibetan edition
chos mngon pa'i mdzod kyi tshig le'ur byas pa. P5590, vol. 115.
French translation
Louis de la Vallée Poussin. *L'Abhidharmakośa de Vasubandhu*. 6 vols. Bruxelles: Institut Belge des Hautes Études Chinoises, 1971.
English translation from the French
Pruden, Leo M. *Abhidharmakośabhāṣyam*. 4 vols. Freemont, CA.: Asian Humanities Press, 1988-89.

Vātsyāyana, Mallanāga. *Kāmasūtra*.
English translations
Bandhu, Acharya Vipin Chandra. *Vātsyāyana's Kāmasūtra (an ancient Indian Classic); The Hindu Art of Love with Oriental*

Illustrations. Foreword by B. P. L. Bedi. Delhi: Universal Publications, 1973.

Burton, Sir Richard and Arbuthnot, F. F. *The Kama Sutra of Vatsyayana*. Ed. with preface by W. G. Archer. Intro. by K. M. Panikkar. London: George Allen and Unwin, 1963; New York: The Berkeley Publishing Group, 1966.

Burton, Sir Richard, *The Kama Sutra of Vatsyayana*. Foreword by John W. Spellman. Intro. by Santha Rama Rau. New York: Penguin/Arkana, 1991.

MacRae, David. *The Kāma Sūtra: Erotic figures in Indian Art*. Presented by Marc de Smedt. New York: Crescent Books, n.d.

Rangaswami Iyengar, K. *The Kāma Sūtra of Vātsyāyana*. Lahore: Punjab Sanskrit Book Dept, 1921.

Sinha, Indra. *The Love Teachings of Kama Sutra: With extracts from Koka Shastra, Anangra Ranga and other famous Indian works on love*. London: Hamlyn, 1980; rpt. 1988.

Upadhyaya, S. C. *Kama Sutra of Vatsyayana*. Foreword by Moti Chandra. Bombay: Taraporevala, 1961; rpt. 1990.

German translation

Schmidt, Richard. *Das Kāmastram des Vātsyāyana, die Indische Ars Amatroia nebst dem Vollständigen Kommentare (Jayamaṅgalā) des Yaśodhara*. Berlin: Hermann Barsdorf Verlag, 1920.

French translation

Liseux, Isidore. *Les Kama sutra de Vatsyayana*. Paris: I. Liseux et ses amis, 1885.

Vīrabhadra. *Kandarpacuḍāmaṇi*. Ed. by R. Sastri Kusala. Lahore: 1926.

White, David. *Myths of the Dog-Man*. Chicago: University of Chicago Press, 1991.

Yön-den-gya-tso (*yon tan rgya mtsho*). *gdong lan lung rig thog mda'*. Paris: 1977.

Yuthok, Dorje Yudon. *House of the Turquoise Roof*. Ithaca: Snow Lion Publications, 1990.